Gandhi–A Humanistic Model

Gandhi

A Humanistic Model

Dr. Ch. Prema Kumar

AKANSHA PUBLISHING HOUSE
NEW DELHI • GUWAHATI • VISAKHAPATNAM

AKANSHA PUBLISHING HOUSE
4649-B/21, Ansari Road
Darya Ganj, New Delhi - 110 002
Ph.: 23263193 / 9811582579 / 09435116718
Fax: 011-23263193
Email: ektabooks@yahoo.com
www.akanshapublishinghouse.com

Gandhi: A Humanistic Model

First Published 2010
ISBN 978-81-8370-238-6

PRINTED IN INDIA

Published by Akansha Publishing House, New Delhi and Printed at Harmain Offset Press, Delhi.

To

My beloved Father
CHIKILE VISWESWARA RAO
and
My Mother CHIKILE SIROMANI
with deepest respects.

Contents

Foreword

Mahatma Gandhi was a multifaceted genius who applied his mind to a large number of human concerns and left an indelible impact on the social, economic and political forces. Gandhi's ideas are becoming more and more relevant with the passing of time.

Gandhi always spoke and understood the language of the masses. He made the people fearless to fight injustice and exploitation. Not only that he wrote, spoke and worked for the various worldly question, viz., full employment, cooperative farming, nutrition and health, communal harmony, value education, upliftment of women, removal of untouchability, environmental problem etc. whenever there is a problem we can get the solution through Gandhian technique. His life was a mission. In fact, throughout his life, he worked for the upliftment of the downtrodden. He practiced what he preached.

Gandhi discusses the function of religion in human society. He believes that religion has different roles to play in different societies. In his approach to economic development, Gandhiji was primarily concerned with the development of starving dumb millions, downtrodden and socio-economically backward people. He argues that if the Gandhian approach for the development of economy on a decentralized way is adopted it would also need a change in the present system of education and training.

Today the participation of an ordinary citizen is confined only to casting vote in favour of a representative or the broad policy of a political party. If the people do not like its performance they can change their choice only in the next elections. He concludes that in order to make the power of the people a reality, in democracy, a ray of hope can be envisaged by bearing in mind Gandhi's ideas about foundation and the institutional basis of democracy. Vasant Nargolkar argues that the greatest need so far as bringing about an improvement in the type of parliamentary government that we have today is decentralization of political and economic power in the country. If the Gram Panchayats, the Zilla Parishads and the State Assemblies are entrusted with more and more self-government, many of the ills of the present system will automatically disappear.

The author in this book has tried to examine the central principles of Gandhian thought on economics, politics, and social reform and proved their relevance to the New World Order. I wish him all the best in his future endeavours.

Andhra University
Visakhapatnam

Prof. SDA Joga Rao
Head Department of Philosophy

Preface

The purpose of this book is to provide an introduction to the "GANDHI – A HUMANISTIC MODEL" related to the human values. The philosophy of Mahatma Gandhi not only influenced greatly the Indian National movement but also inspired movements. His philosophy gave right guidance and direction to some leaders of Human Rights. Gandhi was the defender of human values and human rights and the human equality lakhs of people who were subject to the racial discrimination and colour prejudices to fight non-violently to achieve their objectives and rights. His technique of non-violent resistance and civil disobedience, the exploited human values, and human rights could be taught to use the weapon of non-violent resistance against oppression and injustice. The success tht could be achieved through violence is temporary but the evil it does is permanent. The good that non-violence does is permanent and enduring.

A number of people have read and critically evaluated earlier drafts of the manuscript. I am especially grateful for the profound and honest comments and sincere thanks to Prof. SDA Joga Rao, Head, Department of Philosophy for having kindly consented to write the foreword. Finally I want to thank my wife Ch. Indira for her great support and encouragement, during the period I worked on this manuscript.

Dr. Ch. Prema Kumar

Acknowledgements

I offer my humble gratitude to my parents Sri Chikile Visweswar Rao, Smt. Ch. Siromani, for their blessings. I am grateful to Prof. B. Satyanarayana garu, Vice-Chancellor, Andhra University for his kind support. I would like to thank Prof. L.K. Mohana Rao, Principal, Colleges of Arts and Commerce for his kind blessings.

I am also thankful to the all other faculty members Prof. S. Satyanarayana, Director, Center for Religious Studies, Prof. P. George Victor, Director, Special Assistance Programme and Chairman, Board of Studies, Prof. S.D.A. Jogarao, Head of the Department, Prof. G. Veerraju, Deputy Director, Center for Religious Studies, Prof. K.R. Rajani, Dr. BVS. Bhanusree, Sri. B. Ravibabu, Dr. K. John Christopher, Dr. Ch. Subba Rao, Mr. J. Srinivsa Rao for their cooperation.

I owe a deep sense of gratitude to my family members, Ch. Indira, Ch. Anu Sree Prem, Ch. Rajakumar raju, Ch. Neelima, Ch. Aruna Kumari, Ch. Ratnam Raju, Ch. Krishna Vamsi, Ch. Karishna Prudhevi, Ch. Prudhevi raju, for their support.

My heartiest thanks are to my brother in-law B. Suresh Kumar (Assistant Divisional Engineer) for his support and valuable suggestions to me.

Last but not the least, I express my gratefulness to Shri M.P. Misra, Akansha Publishing House, New Delhi for evincing keen interest in the project and bringing out it elegantly in the present shape.

Dr. Ch. Prema Kumar

Introduction

As we grow up, become educated, and secure for ourselves a place within the social fabric, almost all of us acquire certain general patterns of thought that form what is commonly called a worldview. The process of acquiring a worldview occurs almost entirely unreflectively. We are consciously aware of forming many of our beliefs, but the ways in which these beliefs are arranged and structured into a global framework of understanding is a process that largely occurs sublimely and without careful examination.

However, once acquired, Gandhian views are triply potent within our lives. First, they provide a set of assurances about what is *true*—and especially, they include certain general and fundamental truths that provide us with a way of assessing and fitting together more garden-variety claims into a coherent picture of the human society. Second, they provide the strategies and means of *explaining and understanding* the features of the human behavior that interest us. Third, views typically play an important role in providing us with our social identity. To a greater extent than we may realize, of Gandhi's views mark off social boundaries, distinguishing between a like-minded "we," who share a Gandhi views, from "them," who do not. Thus a human view can function as a kind of entrance ticket to full admission in a social group, society, or human values of Gandhi.

Gandhi says therefore highly prized and, ordinarily, tenacious. Much is at stake in the adoption of a human behavior —and in converting from one view to another, a process that is often wrenching both socially and intellectually. Because of this, it is all the more striking (and worrying) that we often seem to drift into acceptance of an initial human society so casually. But there is a remedy. It is the central mission of philosophy to ask the probing questions that may force us to scrutinize our beliefs to determine whether they can meet basic standards of intellectual rigor. Moreover, it is the special penchant of philosophy to ask these searching questions about *fundamental* beliefs—the sorts of beliefs that constitute the structural girders and foundation stones of Gandhi views.

This book is an introduction to that cluster of ideas and issues that constitute the historical legacy and ongoing projects of a movement. known as humanism. These ideas are characteristically framework ideas: ideas concerning the basic nature of the physical universe, the place and value of human life within it, the proper ends and goals of a life well lived, the proper places within such a life of reason, empirical knowledge, faith, desire, and action, and the nature of those social institutions that permit humans to flourish.

Where they raise methodological questions, these issues force us to think about epistemology the study of human beings as would-be knowers of their world. What are the means by which we can come, not merely to believe, but properly to know that certain things are true? Are these means content-independent, or are they sensitive to the sort of knowledge we seek? Do they depend, for example, upon whether the knowledge in question is knowledge of the physical world, or of mathematics, or of human values, or of supernatural things? And how reliable are the means we have at our disposal.

Gandhi it raises substantive questions, the humanist tradition forces us to think about metaphysics, which concerns the most basic categories of existence—matter, minds, space-time, and qualities—about science, and about religion. It forces us to think about how the human is put together. Is the Gandhi views purely the product of natural forces, or does its structure bespeak the craftsmanship of some supernatural intelligence? How do the laws of nature bear upon human behavior and ascription of moral responsibility? How, in general, is consciousness connected to bodily existence.

The special approach that Gandhi have taken is to discuss these traditional philosophical problems in the context of an engaging journey through the history of humanistic thought. We tend nowadays to think of humanism as *secular* humanism, but it has not always been secular. What distinguishes humanism is the central role it accords to concern about human beings and the requisites for human flourishing. There have been religious humanisms as well as secular ones.

Nevertheless, humanism—secular humanism—has come to be seen, at least within the contemporary culture of the States, as an alternative ideology. Indeed, it is considered the chief ideological rival to religion. Those who use the unfortunate metaphor "culture wars" to describe this rivalry tend to see modern Western culture as polarized into two opposing and irreconcilable camps, and secular humanism as the other. This oversimplification, which is more harmful than helpful, illustrates the need for a greater understanding of both positions and their histories. This book contributes to that goal of Gandhi—a humanistic model.

The bunker mentality reflected in the culture-wars metaphor has fostered some peculiar and sometimes outlandish claims by partisans on both sides. Each party tends to see itself as a besieged minority; each claims to find evils spawned by the opposing ideology to exert pervasive influence upon modern culture. Humanists as a group have been accused of racism, militarism, narrow-minded jingoism, the worst sins of capitalism and anti environmentalism, moral hypocrisy, and more. At the feet of secular humanism (and its supposed allies, Darwinism and metaphysical naturalism) has been laid responsibility for everything from the high divorce rate to illegal drug use, rejection of basic moral principles, mass murder, sexual deviance, the welfare state, and even love of rock music.

Gandhian ideas have consequences, so the saying goes, but what consequences? That is an empirical question, and those that make the sorts of claims just mentioned rarely have any good evidence to support their conclusions; often they do not even care about such niceties. Perhaps they believe that the connections between the ideas and their purported consequences are just "intuitive." The beginning of a corrective for this irresponsible naivete is to acquire an accurate and thorough grasp of the ideas themselves. That is the business of this book. The empirical studies required to both determine the degree of penetration of various ideas into our culture and establish causal connections between their acceptance and one or another social condition is a matter proper to careful sociological analysis in human nature.

This book provides an accessible but fairly comprehensive overview of humanist positions and arguments concerning the centrally disputed issues that have fueled the debate. It also provides a fair summary of major arguments from opponents of humanism. Understanding these arguments will give the reader a better basis for evaluating the culture wars and provide an excellent introduction to the broader arena of philosophical debate. It is to be hoped that some readers will be stimulated to pursue at greater length the important questions.

Finally this book purports to examine certain humanist ideas to determine if there is any justification for accepting or rejecting them. A fair question then is this: What is the justification for *that* idea? That is, what are the grounds for even thinking that humanist can be scrutinized in this way. After all, there is no universally accepted definition of humanism. In fact, there are several competing, restrictive definitions. People usually recognize the need for something like a definition because the term "humanism," like or humanistic model "democracy" or "realism," has been used in more senses than we would care to count. Because of this lack of a common definition, there is a temptation to think that there is no fact of the matter regarding the nature of humanism and human behavior.

Furthermore, Gandhi modern humanist would claim that the very notion of breaking humanism down into distinct statements for easy analysis is wrongheaded. They might say that Gandhian views and ideas are not a set of propositions at all, but an attitude toward life, a way of viewing the world construed in differed ways in different eras. Some might even say that human values defies analysis because it, above all, is neither creed nor dogma.

Even among those who say that humanism does have propositional content and agree more or less on what that content is, there are many differences in emphasis, focus, and implication. The picture gets even fuzzier when we consider that other perspectives that seem clearly non-humanist share many of the ideas that we have labeled humanistical Gandhi.

There is more than an ounce of truth in all of these claims. So how can we even presume to assess "humanist ideas" or to trace the paths of "humanism" through history. How can we dissect a creature we cannot see.

1

Influences on Mahatma Gandhi

Many persons–lay as well as enlightened one have greatly influenced Mohandas Karamchand Gandhi turning him to Mahatma Gandhi. Basically, Mahatma Gandhi was open minded. He was willing to adopt any idea from any source. He was influenced by a number of persons and intellectuals ranging from house-maid Rambha to eminent thinker and writer like Tolstoy. Gandhi was very much influenced by his parents. His mother Putlibai, a lady of most devout temperament influenced his religious thought.

"The outstanding impression" says Gandhi, "my mother has left on my memory is that of saintliness. She was deeply religious. She would not think of taking her meals without daily prayers".[1]

His mother Putlibai had strong commonsense'.[2] He learnt the Indian maxim that 'there is nothing higher than truth' from his mother. He has also learnt that a state of harmlessness or non-violence is the highest religion and a supreme duty 'Ahimsa Paramadharma' from his mother.[3]

Gandhi learnt a lot from his father, Kaba Gandhi. He says that "his rich experience of practical affairs stood him in good stead in the solution of the most intricate questions and in managing hundreds of men".[4]

Gandhi recalled the affection he had obtained from his old nurse. When he had the fear of ghosts and spirits, it was Rambha who suggested to repeate the name of Rama as a remedy for his fear. He considered the name of Rama as an infallible remedy for him.[5] The seed of faith in God that was at work was sown by his nurse Rambha.[6]

Gandhi has developed passion for truth since his childhood. He writes in his autobiography that the passion for truth was innate in me.[7] In support of this, Gandhi quoted an incident which occurred at the examination during his first year at the high school. He could never learn the art of copying although his teacher tried to prompt him.

Gandhi referred to other two incidents which have always clung to his memory and shaped his thought. The first was the book on *Shravana Pitribhakti Nataka* (a play about Shravana's devotion to his parents). He read it with intense interest. He also saw a picture of Shravana Kumar carrying by means of slings fitted for his shoulders, his blind parents on a pilgrimage. The book and the picture of Shravana left an indelible impression on his mind. He said to himself that here was an example for him to copy. The agonized lament of his parents over the death of Shravana was fresh in his memory.[8] This impression has given rise to render service to the humanity.

Another important effect on Gandhi's life was the play of *Harischandra* which captured his heart. He could never be tired of seeing it. He asked himself day and night the question 'why should not all be truthful like Harischandra? To follow truth and to go through all the ordeals, Harishchandra went through was the one ideal that inspired him. He literally believed the story of Hari shchandra. For Gandhi both Hari shchandra and Shravana are living realities.[9]

The influence of the country is noticeable which advocates truth and non-violence. Jainism exerted profound influence on Gandhi. Jainism has been a great living force in Gujarat. He read the teachings of Jainas and also *Saddarsana Samuccya*, the philosophical text of Haribhadra Suriji. Jainism lays more stress on non-violence which impressed Gandhi very much.

Pyarelal has pointed out:

> Three things in the Jaina system of thought influenced Gandhiji's outlook most. They were 'ahimsa on the religious side' *anekantavad* or *syadvad* (the doctrine of may be) on the philosophical side and the institutions of vows on the ethical side. He was greatly attracted too by the Jaina theory of knowledge.[10]

Non-violence is not a negative virtue or a mere mechanical abstention from violence for *Jaina Shastras* but it is a positive quality based on universal love resulting from the recognition of oneness of life and kinship of all living beings. The moment one realizes this, he cannot be indifferent to the suffering of others.[11]

Gandhi has read the Edwin Arnold's book, *The Light of Asia* which is dedicated to the life of Lord Buddha. This book gave him a clear impression about Buddha's teachings. "Look at Gautama's Compassion" Gandhi says, "It was not confined to mankind, it was extended to all living beings".[12]

Buddha says,

> 'Victory breeds hatred, for the conquered is unhappy'.[13]

Both Jainism and Buddhism lay more stress on non-violence, celibacy, non-possession and non-stealing. Of the books that influenced Gandhi's thought and ideas, *Gita* can be ranked first. It has become an infallible guide of conduct and a dictionary of daily references.[14] The teachings of *Gita* especially the verses 62 and 63 of the second chapter have made a deep impression on him.

They read as follows:

> "If one ponders on the objects of the sense, the springs Attraction, from attraction, grow desire. Desire flames to fierce passion, passion breeds Recklessness then the memory - all betrayed - Lets noble purpose go and sap? the mind, Till purpose, mind and roan are all undone."[15]

This book has struck him as of priceless worth. He regarded it as the book par excellence for the knowledge of truth. It has afforded invaluable help in his moments of gloom.[16] No other book influence Gandhi as great as *Bhagavad Gita*. He learnt a great deal about *aparagrah* (non-possession) and *Sambhava* (equability) from *Gita* which have gripped him.[17]

He understood by the *Gita* teaching of non-possession would mean that those who desire salvation should act as the trustees. Although they have control over great possessions they regard not an iota of them as their own. It became clear to him as day light that non-possession and equality presupposed a change of heart and a change of attitude.

Gandhi went through the secrets of the sacred book like *Ramayana* of Tulasidas, the *Mahabharata* of Vyasa, the *Manusmriti* of Manu. Gandhi used the term 'religion' in its broad sense which meant self-realization or knowledge of the self.[18]

The belief that renunciation is the highest form of 2 religions appealed to him greatly.[19]

The reading of the *Ramayana* left a deep impression on Gandhi. He regarded the *Ramayana* of Tulasidas as the greatest book in all devotional literature. Tulasidas advised the sant (the good) to shun the *asant* (evil doer).[20] He held that truth would assert itself in the end.[21] The influence that *Mahabharata* exerted on the life of Mahatma Gandhi cannot be minimized. He says 'I have maintained in the teeth of orthodox Hindu opposition that *Mahabharata* is a book written to establish the futility of war and violence.[22] The better human life is attainable only by means of Non-violence.

Gandhi applied the Edward Maitland's method of allegorical interpretation of the gospels of the Indian Epics. The *Ramayana* and *Mahabharata* and the *Gita* which he insisted should not be regarded as historical works but philosophical poems that are presented in a historical setting. Gandhi was taken up by the Maitland's insistence on 'reasoned faith and later he declared that faith transcends reason but it must not contradict reason.[23]

Gandhi was greatly influenced by the life and teachings of Swami Vivekananda. His conception of *Daridra-narayan*, the God of the poor had been adopted, elaborated and practised by Gandhi himself. Gandhi says,

> *Daridranarayan* is one of the millions of names by which humanity knows God who is unnamable and unfathomable by human understanding and it means, God of the poor God appearing in the hearts of the poor.[24]

Swami Vivekananda humanized the concept of God. He stated that service to the poor is service to God. This must have rather made Gandhi to say:

> I had made the religion of service my own, as I felt that God could be realized only through service. And service for me was the service of India.[25]

Raichandbhai, a saintly Indian merchant and a distinguished reformer of Bombay exerted profound influence on Gandhi. Gandhi pointed out:

> I have since met many a religious leader or teacher. I have tried to meet the heads of various faiths and I must say that no one else has ever made on me the

> impression that Raichandbhai did. His words went straight home to me. His intellect compelled as great a regard from me as his moral earnestness and deep down in me was the conviction that he would never willingly lead me astray and would always confide to me his inner most thoughts. In my moments of spiritual crisis, therefore, he was my refuge.[26]

Raichandbhai moulded Gandhi's thoughts and ideas. He guided Gandhi on many occasions.

Gandhi was greately influenced by Dadabhai Naoroji who was the founder of the Indian National Movement. He was a journalist, economist and a passionate advocate of education for women. He was the first and foremost among Congress patriarchs. As an ardent social reformer and supporter of the temperance movement, he had led an uncompromising crusade against the illegal and immoral opium trade and tirelessly laboured to create organized public life in India for forty years before the birth of Congress. He was thrice elected as the President of the Indian National Congress and lived to be universally revered by his countrymen as the Grand Old Man of India.[27]

Gandhi learnt the first lesson of *ahimsa* (non-violence) from Dadabhai Naoroji. As Romain Rolland apty puts it:

> It was Dadabhai who is trying to moderate Gandhi's youthful ordour, gave him in 1892 his first lesson in *ahimsa* by teaching him to apply heroic passivity - if two such words may be linked to public life by fighting evil, not by evil but by love.[28]

There is no doubt that Gandhi was very much influenced by Dadabhai Naoroji as his saying confirms it.

Dadabhai Naoroji says Gandhi,

> "I am . . . in experienced and young . . . .
> guide me . . . Indians look
> children to the father.[29]

Gopalkrishna Gokhale was an economist, parliamentarian and statesman whose budget speeches have been studied as classics on the subject, whose advise Morley valued and whom Curzon feared and respected as a worthy foe man. He was the founder of Servants of India Society who spurning wordly prospects, would dedicate themselves wholly to the service of the Mother land. It was Gokhale who gave to India the mantra "Politics must be spiritualized".[30] Gandhi proclaimed him as his 'political guru'.

Gokhale exerted considerable influence on Gandhi. Gokhale could bring politics and religion together and I spiritualise politics. Gandhi learnt about the purity of means for the attainment of good from him.

> "Gokhale taught me" says, Gandhi, "that the dream of every Indian who claims to love his country should be not to glorify in language but to spiritualize the political life of the country and the political institutions of the country. He inspired my life and is still inspiring and in that I wish to purify myself and spiritualize myself. I have dedicated myself to that ideal.[31]

The other great Indians who stimulated the young mind of Gandhi were Lokamanya Bal Gangadhar Tilak and Pherozeshah. Tilak, the celebrated author of the *Gita Bahasya* was about daring man of action, a skilled organizer and a born leader of men deeply respected by his admirers and antagonists alike for his personal purity, renunciation and self-sacrifice. He brought the Indian masses into the political field. He had the courage to give voice unhesitatingly to his convictions in spite of all the bureaucratic thunder and he was ever ready to suffer for it. He gave to India the mantra of freedom - 'Swaraj is my birth-right and I shall have it" to which Gandhi later added the other half, viz., "the means are truth and non-violence".[32]

Tilak as an ardent nationalist stood against the interference of the foreign government in the country's affairs especially in social matters. He held that while persuction must be the weapon of the choice in social reform, in politics, compulsion might be necessary.[33] Before Gandhi preached his gospel of non-cooperation, Tilak had set before the nation the entire programme of non-cooperation.[34]

The other great person who shaped the thought of Gandhi was Sir Pherozeshah. He was in legal profession before he joined the Congress. After his return from South Africa, Gandhi had chosen Bombay as the first city to educate public (opinion) relating to the problems of the Indians settled in South Africa. Gandhi tried to ventilate their grievances through pamphlets.

> "Sir Pherozeshah", says Gandhi, "had seemed to me like the Himalayas, the Lokamanya like the ocean. But Gokhale was as the Ganges. One could have a refreshing bath in the holy river. The Himalayas was unscalable, and one could not easily launch forth on the sea, but the Ganges invited me to its bosom".[35]

Western Influence

Although Gandhi was an Indian, he was deeply influ-enced by the Western thinkers, writers, prophets of both the ancient and modern. Gandhi himself acknowledged his indebtedness to the West. He did not think that every-thing western has to be rejected. He learnt something about *ahimsa* from the west.

> "I have nothing to be ashamed of" says Gandhi,"if my views on ahimsa (non-violence) are the result of my Western education. I have never tabooed all western ideas nor am I prepared to anathematize everything that comes from the west are inherently evil. I have learnt much from the West and I should not be surprised to find that I had learnt something about ahimsa too from the West."[36]

The ancient Greek philosopher Socrates exerted profound influence on Gandhi as a seeker of truth. About Socrates Gandhi pointed out:

> Socrates would not refrain from preaching what he knew to be Truth to the Athenian Youth and bravely suffered the punishment of death. He was in his case a Satyagrahi.[37]

Gandhi admired the courage of Socrates who preferred a cup of poision to give up his pursuit of truth. Socrates resisted the superstitoous beliefs of his people through the non-violent means.

The *New Testament* especially the Sermon on the Mount had influence Gandhi which went straight to his heart. Gandhi quoted Jesus' saying written in *New Testament* Matthew 5th chapter - 39th and 40th verses -

> But I say unto you, that ye resist not evil, but whosoever shall smite thee on thy right cheek turn to him the other also. And if any man takes away thy coat let him have thy cloak too.[38]

These verses delighted Gandhi beyond measure. He tried to unify the teachings of Gita the Light of Asia with the Sermon on the Mount.[39] He found the spirit of renunciation present in the Sermon on the Mount which appealed to him greatly.

> "I have not been", says Gandhi, "able to see any difference between the Sermon on the Mount and the *Bhagavad Gita*. What the Sermon describes in a graphic manner the *Bhagavad Gita* reduces to a scientific formula. It may not be a scientific ftar in the accepted sense of the term, but it has argued out of the law of love the law of abandon as I could call it in a scientific manner. The Sermon on the Mount gives the same law in wonderful language. The *New Testament* gave me comfort and boundless joy as it came after the

> repulsion that parts of the old has given me. Today supposing I was deprived of the *Gita* and forgot all its contents but I had a copy of the Sermon, I should derive the same joy from it as I do from the *Gita.*[40]

For Gandhi Jesus was one of the greatest teachers humanity has ever had. He believed that Jesus does not belong solely to Christianity alone, but to the entire world and all races and people.[41] Gandhi wondered at the Christ's non-violent character. He called Jesus as 'the Prince of Satyagrahis'. In England Gandhi renewed the study of the *Bible.* He said that Jesus played a great part in his life. He felt the beauty of the Sermon on the Mount while reading it. He said that so many words were chosen from the Bible. He could not avoid referring to *Bible* in his talks. He had immesurable love for Christ.

Theosophy believes that all religions are the branches of one religion. Gandhi read Madame Blavatsky's Key to Theosophy at the instance of the Theosophist brothers.[42] He was also introduced to the literature of other religions. He advocated the view that even as a tree has a single trunk, it has many branches and leaves. Similarly the true religion becomes many and passes through the human medium. He felt that the creed of truth and non-violence cannot be denied by any religion.

Tolstoy left a deep spiritual impression on Gandhi. Tolstoy's book *'the Kingdom of God is Within You'* has overwhelmed him which has left an abiding impression on Gandhi.[43]

Gandhi said that Tolstoy was the best and brightiest exponent of the doctrine of passive resistance. Tolstoy not only expounded it but also lived in accordance with it.[44]

> "When I was passing through", says Gandhi, "a severe crisis of scepticism and doubt that I came across his book, the Kingdom of God is Within You and was deeply

> impressed by it. I was at that time a believer in violence. Its reading cured me of my scepticism and made me a firm believer in *ahimsa* (Non-violence) what has appealed to me most in Tolstoy's life is that he practised what he preached and reckoned no cost too great in his pursuit of truth.[45]

Tolstoy founded all governments being based on violence and force. According to Tolstoy the only social order must be based on love and persuation but not on violence. Gandhi stated that after making an intensive study of the Tolstoy books, *The Gospels in Brief* and other books made a deep impression on him. He began to realize more and more the infinite possibilities of universal love.[46]

Love could be found as the sovereign principle in Tolstoy's doctrine which is rooted in the Gospel Text 'Resist not him that is evil'. Tolstoy laid more stress on the moral regeneration of the individual. He opposed the use of force.

Gandhi considered Tolstoy as one of his good teachers. He pointed out about Tolstoy:

> There is no doubt that there is nothing new in what Tolstoy preaches. But his presenta-tion of the Old Truth is refreshingly forceful. His logic is unassailable. And, above all, he endeavours to practise what he preaches. He preaches to convince. He is sincere and earnest. He commands attention.[47]

Gandhi was attracted towards the concept of breed-labour. It was first enunciated by a Russian writer named TM. Bondaref and was much advertised by Tolstoy.

Next to Tolstoy was Ruskin, the other modern writer. His writings exerted profound influence on Gandhi. Mr. Polak an European with whom Gandhi made acquaintance in the vegetarian restaurant came to see him off at the station. Mr. Polak left with Gandhi a book to read during the journey. It was Ruskin's *Unto This Last*. The book was impossible to lay aside once he began it. It gripped him. It brought about an instantaneous and practical transformation in the life of Gandhi. He translated it later into Gujarati entitling it *Sarvodaya* (the welfare of all).

Gandhi discovered that some of his deepest convictions reflected in that Great book of Ruskin. lhat is why that book captured and transformed the life of Gandhi.

The teachings of *Unto This Last* as Gandhi understood to be:

1. That the good of the individual is contained in the good of all.
2. That a lawyer's work has the same value as the barbers, in as much as all have the same right of earning their livelihood from their work.
3. That a life of labour, i.e., the life of the tiller of the soil and handicraftsman is the life worth living.

Gandhi decided to put these principles into practice. He said that first of these, he knew, the second he had dimily realized, but the third had never occurred to him. Unto This Last made it clear as day light for him that the second and third were contained in the first.[49]

Gandhi felt that if mankind were to progress and to realize the ideal of equality and brotherhood, it must adopt and act on the principle of Unto This Last.Both Gandhi and Ruskin shared the common views. They stood against the western civilization though not against the people of the west. Both stood against the craze for machinery. Both were common in their views on educational, economic and political problems. Gandhi drew his inspiration on education from Ruskin. Both of them attached importance to education and constructive programmes.

Henry David Thoreau

Henry David Thoreau, the well known American

anarchist influenced Gandhi. Gandhi read Thoreau's book on Civil Disobedience with great interest when he was imprisoned due to the *Satyagraha* campaign in South Africa. Gandhi defined Civil Disobedience as 'civil breach of immoral statutory enactments without the fear of its sanctions.[50]

Gandhi said that the weapon of Civil Disobedience is of dreadful type meant mainly to be used against the states. This expression was coined by Henry David Thoreau to signify his own resistance to the laws of a slave state. Thoreau had left a masterly treatise on the duty of Civil Disobedience. Gandhi did not consider Thoreau to be out and out champion of Civil Disobedience. Thoreau appears to have limited his breach of statutory laws to the revenue law i.e., payment taxes but Gandhi covered the breach to any statutory and immoral. It signifies the resisters outlaw in a civil i.e., in a non-violent manner.[51] Thoreau also influenced Gandhi on the nature and functions of the state.

Gandhi says:

> To me political power is not an end but one of the means of enabling people to better than condition in every department of life. Political power means capacity to regulate national life through national representatives. If national life becomes so perfect as to become self-regulated, no representation becomes necessary. There is then a state of enlightened anarchy. In such a state everyone is his ruler. He rules him-self in such a manner that he is never a hindrance to his neighbor. In the ideal state, therefore, there is no political power because there is no state. But the ideal is never fully realized in life. Hence the classical statement of Thoreau that that government is best that governs the least.[52]

Islamic Influence

Islamic religion has played an important role in shaping the religious views of Mahatma Gandhi. The personal character of Prophet Mohammad, Hazrat Ali, and Imam

Hussain influenced Gandhi on a large measure. Gandhi regarded this religion as a religion of peace for sword is not the emblem of Islam. Gandhi found the teachings of Prophet Mohammad in consonance with ahimsa.[53]

Gandhi interpreted Islam as a religion which believes in the brotherhood of man but not the brotherhood of Muslims alone. This concept of universal brotherhood, he said led him to non-violence. He often quoted from Koran and Zend Avesta in the prayer meetings. Gandhi drew the inspiration from the East and the West.[54]

REFERENCES

1. M.K. Gandhi. *The Story of My Experiments with Truth*, p. 2.
2. *Ibid.* p. 3.
3. D.M. Datta. *The Philosophy of Mahatma Gandhi*, p. 9.
4. M.K. Gandhi. *The Story of My Experiments with Truth*. p. 2.
5. *Ibid.* p. 23.
6. *Ibid.* p. 34.
7. *Ibid.*
8. *Ibid.* p. 7.
9. *Ibid.* p.4
10. *Ibid.*
11. Pyarelal. *Mahatma Gandhi - The Early Phase. Vol. I*, p. 276..
12. *Ibid.* p. 276.
13. M.K. Gandhi. *The Story of My Experiments with Truth*, p.120.
14. Coomaraswamy and Horner. *Gautama the Buddha*, p.122.
15. M.K. Gandhi. *The Story of My Experiments with Truth*, 198
16. *Ibid*, p. 50.
17. *Ibid.*
18. *Ibid.*, p. 198.*Ibid*, p.198
20. *Ibid.*, p. 198.
21. *Young India*, 4-8-1920. p.4
22. *Young India*, 3-1-1929, p.6

23. N.B. Sen (ed.). *Wit and Wisdom of Mahatma Gandhi*, p. 146.
24. Pyarelal, *Mahatma Gandhi*, Vol.I, *The Early Phase*, p.324.
25. U.S. Mchan Rao (ed). *The Message of Mahatma Gandhi*, p.12.
26. M.K. Gandhi. *The Story of My Experiments with Truth*, p. 118.
27. *Ibid.*, pp. 64-65.
28. Pyarelal. *Mahatma Gandhi. Vol.1*, Navajeevan Publishing House, Ahmedabad, 1965, p.128.
29. Romain Rolland, *Mahatma Gandhi*
30. Pyarelal. *Mahatma Gandhi*. Vol. I, p 138
31. *Ibid.*, p.139.
32. M.K. Gandhi. *In Search of the Supreme. Vol.11*, p. 3,
33. Pyarelal. *Mahatma Gandhi. Vol.I*, p. 140.
34. *Ibid.*, pp.141-42.
35. D.K. Datta., *Social, Moral and Religious Philosophy of Mahatma Gandhi*, p. 31.
36. M.K. Gandhi, *The Story of My Experiments with Truth*, p. 109.
37. M.K. Gandhi. *Hindu Dharma*, p.199.
38. M.K. Gandhi. *On the Back Flap of The Science of Satyagraha.*
39. M.K. Gandhi, *The Story of My Experiments with Truth*, p. 51.
40. *Ibid*. p. 102..
41. *Young India*. 22.12.1927. p. 426.
42. *The Modern Review*, Oct. 1941, p. 407.
43. M.K. Gandhi. *The Story of My Experiments with Truth*, p.51.
45. *Ibid.*, p.102.
46. *Speeches and Writings of Mahatma Gandhi*, p. 165
47. *Young India*. 20.9.1928, p. 319.
48. M.K. Gandhi. *The Story of My Experiments with Truth*, p.119.
49. M.K. Gandhi, *Collected Works of Mahatma Gandhi. Vol. X*, p.
50. M.K. Gandhi, *The Story of My Experiments with Truth*, p. 224.
51. *Ibid.*, p. 224.
52. *Harijan*, 25.8.1946, p. 281.
53. M.K. Gandhi. *Satyagraha*, pp. 3-4.
54. *Young India*, 2.7.1931, p. 162.

2

Ethics

The word 'ethics' etymologically means a place where people live together. In the passage of time, the word ethics has acquired several meanings including custom, temperament and way of thinking. The history of the word 'ethos' provides an important observation. It relates to the customs and characters of men which emerge in the course of their co-existence. An identity has to be brought about between universal moral standards and man's real behaviour.

History records Mahatma Gandhi as a great leader who has dedicated his entire life for the lofty goal i.e., the liberation of the country from the foreign oppression and domination. The purposefulness of his life reveals the moral values he has held important and throws light on what moral value orientation ought to be. His life goals are marked by moral values. He aroused man's conscience from the slumber. He channeled his efforts into right direction by fighting against cruelty, oppression, despotism and his opposition to the opportunist tactices by vindicating evil by immediate necessity which is opposed to the recognition of the principle 'the end justifies the means'.

Gandhi derived his moral values from his unshakable faith in the unseen mysterious supreme Divine Power which he identified with Truth. The foundations of man's moral and ethical behaviour do not lie in abstract ideas of a transcendental life but are directly connected to real earthly life itself.

Moral values not only do help for the stability of society and the cooperation among its members but they also ennoble man. Man has freedom to reflect and respond to his environment within historical and social limitations. He is free to choose between good and evil, between justice and injustice, between selfishness and selflessness. Man develops his individuality through his own personal efforts, his own talents and skills, his will power and commitment. Only such qualities are capable of shaping and developing the human personality.

Development of human personality does not consist in shunning creative activities and depending on mystic contemplation of the inner self but in ceaseless struggles to remove the causes of sin and evil and free life of all evils, oppression and violence, and to make the conditions conducive for the development of individuality.

This is a process for self-realization which demands an uncompromising struggle to transform social conditions that make the humanity to sink to the depths of deprivation and degradation. It is closely linked with the needs and aspirations of humanity for a better, nobler and happier life on earth free from exploitation, oppression and violence.

Moral principles have no bearing on the human life if considered in the abstract and they can be discussed in the context of the concrete/historical/ social and human situation Mahatma Gandhi demonstrated the practicability of ethical and spiritual life in all the spheres of the human endeavour.

He believed in the moral value of actions undertaken with an effort. He insisted that to achieve good one must be prepared for the suffering. He believed also that whatever is achieved with voluntary suffering with an effort must be good.[1]

Morality for Gandhi is the very foundation of life. The real progress of individual and society depends on morality. Morality keeps in check the passions and impulses that lead to discord and strife and promotes on the other hand feelings that create harmony, peace and happiness. Morality has the greatest survival value which has evolved gradually through the long process of the evolution of man.[2]

Love is the essence of morality which helps the finite individual widen his narrow self and breaks the barriers between himself and others and takes him towards the universal. What the reasoning or threat can not accomplish love can quite spontaneously accomplish. All duties towards fellow beings follow from love and the performance of duty is made pleasant by love. Love penetrates into the every sphere of the human life, turning all impulses into one pleasant or orchestral harmony.[3] Gandhi tried to realize this truth, so he says:

> My life is one indivisible whole and all activities run into one another and they all have their rise in my insatiable love of mankind. Again, for me, the Law of complete Love is the Law of my being.[4]

Knowledge

But love has to be gradually perfected by knowledge and moral effort. Knowledge liberates love from its narrow limits when man is not aware of his real nature, and he is moved by the cravings of the flesh. The moment he realizes his underlying Reality through which an inseparable relation is established with rest of existence, his love does not remain confined to himself but goes beyond the frontiers of his self-interest. Without the realization of Truth, love would be narrow and blind and truth without love would be a mere unrealized ideal. So Mahatma Gandhi lays more stress on the necessity of morality. Any action which is mere mechanical performed with blind impulse or custom is not really moral. Morality implies conscious voluntary action.[5]

> "No action" says Gandhi, "which is not voluntary can be called moral. So long as we act like machines, there can be no question of morality; If we want to call an action moral, it should have been done consciously and as a matter of duty. Any action that is directed by fear or by coercion of any kind ceases to be moral.[6]

A good action requires the knowledge of the conditions of other fellow beings and the situation of the surroundings especially the motives behind the action. Self-examination acquires great importance in the ethics of Gandhi. He holds that one must be one guard and watch the motives that prompt ones action.[7] He pointed out:

> Our desires and motives may be divided into two classes - selfish and unselfish. All selfish desires are immoral while the desire to improve ourselves for the sake of doing good to others is truly moral.[8]

So self analysis is necessary to check our selfish motives. In the absence of self analysis and self-examination, there cannot be self-purification. Whenever Gandhi had any conflict or discord with others, he used to engage himself in the self examination to check his motives and actions. In the event of any mistake on his side, he used to confess and rectify his mistake. His advice was that we must also try to see as others see us. This type of knowledge is essentially good. This leads to a successful and moral life.[9]

Moral Maxims

The following are the moral maxims that Gandhi found them to be useful in day to day life.

The Greatest Good of All

Gandhi does not subscribe to the utilitarian formula 'the greatest good to the greatest number'. His motto was to strive for the greatest good of all and to die in realizing this ideal'. The greatest good of all he says, inevitably includes the good of the greatest number ... the utilitarian to be logical will never sacrifice himself. The absolutist will even sacrifice himself.[10] One whose bases is his moral principle but not selfish search for pleasure, relies on love and reason. He sees his longer interest in the interest of all. His ideal should therefore be the greatest good of all.[11]

Duties But Not Rights

Gandhi holds that we cannot morally acquire the legitimate right either from the State or from society or individuals unless we discharge our duties. If all insist on only rights ignoring duties, there will be utter chaos and confusion. Instead of insisting on rights if everyone does his duty, the rule of moral order will be established. [12]

> "The true source of rights is duty" says Gandhi, "If we all discharge our duties, rights will not be far to seek. If leaving duties unperformed we run after rights, they will escape us like a will-o-the wisp. The more we pursue them, the farther will they fly. The same teaching has been embodied by Krishna in the immortal words - 'Action alone is thine. Leave them the fruit severely alone'. Action is duty; fruit is the right."[13]

Faith on the Goodness of the Individual

Gandhi believed in the goodness of inherent in every individual. He says that it is wise to hate the sin but unwise to hate the sinner. He has faith on the goodness of the individual. He says that the spirit of non-violence lies dormant in the brute.[14]

Means and Ends

If the means adopted is not moral, the end cannot be

moral. All moral means should be utilized to make man morally better and the use of foul means is morally unjustifiable.[15] There has been an inseparable nexus established between the two and they should be equally pure. As some people think that end is high, is not acceptable to Gandhi. For him the means must be as moral as the end. He says that the end cannot justify the means.[16] He pointed out that if one takes care of the means, the end will take care of itself."[17] He further says, "They say means are after all means". I would say 'means are after all everything. As the means so the end, there is no wall of separation between means and end [18]. For Gandhi means and ends are convertible terms.[19]

Gandhi compares means to a seed and end to a tree:

> "The means" says Gandhi, "may be likened to a seed, the end to a tree, and there is just the same inviolable connection between the means and the end as there is between the seed and the tree.[20]

He holds that the realization of the goal is in exact proportion to that means.[21] The opposite theory that ends justifies the means leads to arrive at the conclusion that violent means that are dangerous in practice and ethically unsound can be applied. This gives recourse to resort to violence, untruth and all other evils.[22]

Cardinal Virtues

Though the systems of Indian Philosophy differed one from the other widely on metaphysical questions, unanimity on a great deal is present among them in Ethics. Good work causes good result and bad work results in evil. Gandhi adhered to the moral belief - doing his duty only for duty sake without expecting the result.[23] The general unanimity could be found among the Indian thinkers about the practice of some cardinal virtues such as non-violence which is a state of harmlessness (*ahimsa*), truthfulness (*satya*), non-stealing (*asteya*), chastity (*brahmacharya*), non-possession of unnecessary things (*aparigraha*). These five virtues have been recognized by the *Upanishads*, the Buddhists, the Jainas, the *Yoga* system and most others.[24]

Gandhi has accepted the five traditional virtues and gave a new interpretation in the light of his own experience. To have perfect practice of the cardinal values. Gandhi followed the general Indian formula in thought, speech and deed. This is essentially the teaching of *Bible* also. Purity of life cannot be maintained unless the entire human life of thought speech and deed becomes pure. For Gandhi, Truth is the root of existence and there could be no room for hypocrisy which allows one thing in mind, another in speech and something else in action. Gandhi preferred to take vows to observe the moral laws.[25]

Ahimsa (Non-violence)

Literally non-violence (*ahimsa*) means non-injury and hence non-killing. Gandhi gave a new interpretation to non-violence. He redefined the meaning of non-violence and described it in a new perspective. He said that non-violence in the historical setting is made to appear crude. No doubt to hurt any living being is a part of ahimsa but it is its least expression. The principle of violence is hurt by evil thought, undue haste, lying, hatred and wishing ill-will to anybody.[26]

Gandhi makes a distinction between the positive and the negative meaning of non-violence.

> "*Ahimsa*" says Gandhi, "is not merely a negative state of harmlessness but it is a positive state of love, doing good even to the evil doer. But it does not mean helping the evil-doer to continue the wrong or tolerating it by passive acquiescence. On the contrary, love the active state Ahimsa - requires you to resist the wrong doer by disassociating yourself from him even though it may offend him or injure him physically."[27]

Again he says:

> In its positive form *ahimsa* means the largest love and the greatest charity.[28]

Gandhi conceives non-violence as the law of existence and a moral law Man has to obey to that law for human existence and progress does not lie in violence.

The practice of non-violence proceeds with the basic principle:

> "that what holds good in respect of one self equally applies to the whole universe. All mankind in essence are alike what is possible for one person is possible for everybody.[29]

***Satya* (Truth)**

The word *satya* (truth) is derived from *'Sat'* which means being. Nothing except Truth exists in reality. That where there is truth, there is true knowledge. Where there is true knowledge, there is bless and no place for sorrow it. Truth is eternal and the bliss emanates from it.[30]

Truth is the sovereign principle. Nearest approach to Truth is through love. Truthfulness in thought and deed flows spontaneously from the love of fellow beings, Professing to love a person and deceiving him by words or deeds is contrary to truth. Truth and love are inseparable to Gandhi.[31]

> "But one thing took deep root in me", says Gandhi, "the conviction that morality is the basis of things" and that truth is the substance of all morality. Truth became my sole objective."[32]

Regard for truth results in truthfulness in thought, speech and deed. Truth by nature is self evident when the ignorance is removed, truth shines clear. Search for truth and the experience of truth requires self-examination and self-purification. One cannot experience truth as long as one is under the influence of six deadly enemies namely 'lust, anger, greed, infatuation, pride and falsehood.[33]

> "A devotee of truth" says Gandhi, "may not be any-thing in difference of convention. He must always hold himself open to correction and whenever he discovers himself to be wrong, he must confess it at all cost and alone for it."[34]

Asteya (Non-stealing)

Both Jainism and Buddhism which influenced Gandhi lay more stress on non-stealing and non-possession. Non-stealing is a moral virtue prescribed by Gandhi. The observance of this virtue entails not to take away the property of anyone unless it is given by the latter. It recognizes the right of everyone of his property. The Jaina thinkers point out that the property is 'the outer life, of a person' and to rob him of property is to rob him of his life. A person cannot make his living without the possession. So if any one recognizes it as a duty not to injure his life, he must not rob the other of his possession. This virtue is based on love. For Gandhi, the meaning of non-stealing as a vow is not merely to desist from committing the act of theft but also desisting from all kinds of exploitation at the cost of others such as the capitalists appropriation of the fruits of the labour of the workers. In all such exploitation, Gandhi could find the element of violence present.[35]

Gandhi holds that it is impossible for a person to steal and simultaneously claim to know Truth or cherish Truth. He considers it theft to take something from the other when the person is not in need of it. People multiply their wants improperly and unconsciously become thieves of themselves. Non-stealing brings about a progressive reduction in the wants of man.[36]

Aparigraha (Non-possession)

It is a vow of not possessing everything. Non-possession

implies not o accumulate things not more than necessary for the day. Gandhi says that non-possession is allied to non-stealing. A thing not originally stolen must nevertheless be classified as stolen property if we possess it without the need of it. Possession implies to preserve for the future. A seeker of Truth and a follower of the law of love, cannot hold anything for tomorrow, says Gandhi. Due to the ignorance of the Divine Law, which gives man his daily bread, has given rise to inequalities with all the miseries attendant upon them. The rich have a superfluous, store of things which they do not need but are neglected and wasted while millions are starved to death for want of sustenance.[37]

Gandhi holds that the highest fulfilment of religion is to give up all possessions and to set about to reduce to practice to the extent possible.[38]

Gandhi pointed out:

> Love and exclusive possession can never go together. Theoretically, where there is perfect love, there must be perfect non-possession.

Brahmacharya (Celibacy)

This has also been practised as a cardinal virtue. The word *brahmacharya* carries the meaning search of Brahman. Brahman pervades every being. Therefore he can be searched by diving into and realizing the inner self. But this realization is not possible without complete control of the senses. In the words of Gandhi *brahmacharya* means 'control in thought, word and action, of all the senses at all times and in all places'. A man or woman who practises complete Brahmacharya is absolutely free from passion.[39]

Gandhi holds that a person who appears to control his body, but nurses evil thoughts in his mind makes vain effort.[40]

> "He who attempts" says Gandhi, "to control only one organ and allows all the others free play is bound to find his effort futile."[41]

***Abhaya* (Fearlessness)**

Gandhi added another virtue namely fearlessness to the five cardinal virtues which has been mentioned in the ancient scriptures like *Upanishads.* This is proved to be of much importance as a vow especially for workers who are trained to face death and untold suffering in their non-violent fight against powers armed with deadly weapons.[42]

Gandhi considers moral bravery as the highest heroism which consists not in striking and injuring others but in the readiness to sacrifice, patiently and fearlessly anything and even life for the good of other fellow beings out of love for them.[43]

Gandhi described fearlessness in the following words:

> "Fearlessness connotes freedom from all external fear - fear of disease, bodily injury or death, or dispossession, of losing one's nearest and dearest, of losing reputation or giving offence, and so on."[44]

Gandhi holds that when one is afraid even to do the right thing, there is much superstition and hypocrisy around that. If one gives way to fear, even the truth has to be suppressed. The golden rule is to act fearlessly upon what one believes to be right.[45]

Gandhi says that "perfect fearlessness can be attained only when one has realized the Supreme. It is freedom delusions. One can progress always towards this goal by determined and constant Endeavour and also by increasing confidence in oneself."[46] Gandhi holds that fearlessness does not mean arrogance or aggressiveness which is a sign of fear. The fearlessness presupposes a state of calmness followed by a peace of mind.[47] He says, "let us fear God and we shall cease to fear man."[48] As the coward with the grip of fear is capable of committing any sin coward can never be moral.[49] Gandhi pointed out that fearlessness is a sine qua non for the growth of the other noble qualities. One cannot seek truth or cherish love without fearlessness.[50]

REFERENCES

1. G. Ramachandran (Ed). *Quest For Gandhi*, p. 319.
2. Dhirendra Mohan Datta. *The Philosophy of Mahatma Gandhi*. p. 75.
3. *Ibid.*, p. 76.
4. N.K. Bose, *Selections from Gandhi*, p. 45.
5. Dhirendra Mohan Datta, *op.cit.*, p. 77.
6. Nirmal Kumar Bose, *Selections from Gandhi*, p. 300.
7. D.M. Datta, *op.cit.*, p. 77.
8. Nirmal Kumar Bose, *Selections from Gandhi*, p. 2 23.
9. D.M. Datta, *op.cit.*, p. 78.
10. M.K. Gandhi, *Sarvodaya*. p.4.
11. D.M. Datta, *op.cit.*, pp.82-83.
12. M.K. Gandhi, *Sarvodaya*. p. 6.
13. *Young India*. 8.1.1925. pp. 15-16.
14. *Ibid.*, 11.8.1920, p.3.
15. D.M.Datta, *op.cit.*, p.84.
16. M.K. Gandhi, *Ethical Religion*, p.42.
17. *Karijan*, 11.2.1939. p. 8.
18. Nirmal Kumar Bose, *Selections from Gandhi*, p. 37.
19. M.K. Gandhi, *Hindu Dharma*, p. 5.
20. M.K. Gandhi. *Hind Swaraj*, p. 71.
21. Nirmal Kumar Bose (Ed). *op.cit.*, p.318.
22. Gopinath Dhavan, *The Political Philosophy of Mahatma Gandhi*, p. 55.
23. D.M. Datta, *op.cit.*, pp. 86-87.
24. *Ibid.*, p. 87.
25. *Ibid.*
26. M.K, *Gandhi From Yervda Mandir—Ashram Observances*, p.7.
27. *Young India*, 25.8.1920. p. 2.
28. *Speeches and Writings of Mahatma Gandhi*, p.346.
29. *Harijan*, 28.1.1939. p. 441.

30. H.K. Gandhi, *From Yervda Mandir and Ashram Observances*, p. 2.
31. D.M. Datta, *op.cit.*, p. 97.
32. M.K. Gandhi, *The Story of My Experiments with Truth*, p. 25.
33. M.K. Gandhi, *Hindu Dharma*, p. 240.
34. M.K. Gandhi, *The Story of My Experiments with Truth*, p. 265.
35. D.M. Datta, *op.cit.*, p. 98.
36. M.K. Gandhi, *From Yeravda Mandir and Ashram Observances*, pp. 19-20
37. *Ibid.*, pp. 23-24.
38. *Modern Review*, Oct. 1935, p. 412.
39. *Young India*, 5.6.1924. p. 186.
40. M.K. Gandhi, *From Yeravda Mandir and Ashram Observances*, p.12.
41. *Ibid.*, p.13.
42. D.M. Datta, *op.cit.*, p.103.
43. *Ibid.*, p.103.
44. *Young India*, 11.9.1930. p. 2.
45. *Harijan*, 2.6.1946. p. 160.
46. *Young India*, 11.9.1930. p. 2.
47. *Harijan*, 3.11.1946. p. 388.
48. *Speeches and Writings of Mahatma Gandhi*, p. 130.
49. *Young India*, 13.10.1921. p. 323.
50. *Ibid.*, 2.9.1926. p. 308.

3

Religion

Nature of Religion

Religion is a pervasive and almost a universal phenomenon in the human societies. Although the word 'religion' is used without any hesitation it is difficult to give correct meaning to it. The *Oxford Dictionary* defines it as "Recognition on the part of man of some unseen higher power as having control of his destiny and as being entitled to obedience, reverence and worship". The essence of religion is the belief in the most important values which are in harmony with the enduring structure of the universe.

Gandhi brought down religion from the cloistered seclusion of yogic contemplation to man's socio-political life of clash and conflict. On the other hand, he sought to lift political struggle to the plane of moral and spiritual endeavour.[1] Gandhi defines religion "as a belief in the ordered moral government of the universe".[2] For Gandhi, religion pervades everyone and it is not sectarianism. He holds that religion binds indissolubly to truth and it is a permanent element present in human nature.[3]

Religion and Morality

According to Gandhi, religion provides a moral basis to

all our activities. If the moral content is lacked, the human life becomes meaningless. For Gandhi 'there is no religion higher than Truth and Righteousness.' He does not accept any unreasonable religious sentiments that are not moral. He holds that 'as soon as we lose moral basis, we cease to be religious'.[4] Morality is possible without religion but religion contributes greatly to the growth of morality.

> "True religion" says Gandhi, "and true morality are inseparably bound up with each other. Religion is to morality what water is to the seed that is sown in the soil".[5]

Gandhi considers every aspect of human life from the moral standpoint. His main object is to equalise religion with morality and make religion dynamically operative in the human life.[6] Religion has to integrate various moral aspects of the human life. Ethics is held to be the science of ideals. Gandhi has synthesized religion and ethics for he thinks, that ethics does not preclude religion. True morality does not consist in following the beaten track but in finding the truth and fearlessly following it.[7]

Reason and Religion

If man is able to give sufficient reason for the faith he has, that religion becomes meaningful and purposive. Gandhi does not plead for the suppression of reason.[8] There are subjects of which we cannot give rational explanation. As such of subjects cannot take us far, we have to make room for faith for subjects of this nature.

> "There are subjects" says Gandhi, "where reason cannot take us far and we have to accept things on faith. Faith then does not contradict reason but transcends it. Faith is a kind of sixth sense which works on cases which are without the preview of Reason.[9]

Gandhi on the other hand, declines to be bound by any interpretation, however, learned it may be, if it is repugnant to reason or moral sense.

Religion and Human Life

Gandhi considers the human life as an integral whole which cannot be divided into water-tight compartments—social, economic, political and religious. All act and react upon one another.[10] Religion pervades the entire texture of human life. He believes on the other hand that spiritual law expresses itself through the ordinary activities of human life. [11]

> "If one gains spiritually", says Gandhi, "the whole world gains with him and if one man falls, the whole world falls to that extent.[12]

Gandhi is of the opinion that religion which does not take the practical affairs into consideration and does not help to solve them, is no religion.[13] Gandhi makes the people conscious of His presence and states that the only way to find God is to see Him in His creation and be one with it. As a result the immediate service to all the humanity becomes absolutely necessary. Gandhi could not find God apart from the rest of the human activity.

In order to see the universal and all pervading spirit of Truth face to face, one must be able to love the nearest of the creation as one self.[14] "God" says Gandhi, "is neither in heaven nor down below, but in everyone".[15] Gandhi is aware that "God is found more often in the lowest of His creatures than in the high and mighty".[16] So Gandhi has much concern for the supressed and the oppressed classes. According to him there is "no greater sin than to oppress the innocent in the name of God".[17]

Religion and Truth

Truth is the sovereign principle in which Gandhi includes numerous other principles. Passion for truth is innate in him. This truth is truthfulness in word, thought and deed. It is not alone the relative truth of our conception but the Absolute Truth, the eternal principle which he calls God. He worships

God as Truth. He relies on the relative truth which is within the human reach till such time, he finds the Absolute Truth.

> "But as long as" says Gandhi, "I have not realized this Absolute Truth, so long must I hold by the relative truth as I have conceived it. This relative truth must mean while be my beacon, my shield and buckler." [18]

Gandhi holds that the word Truth (*satya*) is derived from '*sat*' which means "being". Nothing except Truth exists in reality. That is why '*sat*' or 'Truth' is attributed to God. Earlier he has pointed out that God is Truth but later on he states that it is more correct to say that Truth is God than to say God is Truth.[19] Transition in his saying from 'God is Truth to Truth is God' could be found. He maintains that his uniform experience has convinced him that there is no other God than Truth.[20] This led him to state that he would not care for God, if He is anything but Truth, anything but the undeniable reality revealed in man and outside.

For Gandhi, morality constitutes the basis of things and that truth is the substance of all morality and this conviction is deep rooted in him. Truth has become his sole objective,[21] He attributes all social and human values to God.

> "Tome" says Gandhi, "God is Truth and Love. God is ethics and morality. God is fearlessness. God is the source of light and life and yet above and beyond all these God is conscience. He is even the atheism of an atheist... He transcends speech and reason."[22]

Gandhi tries to understand the spirit of the various scriptures of the world. He applies the Test of Truth and non-violence and rejects what is inconsistent with that test and appropriates all that is consistent with[23] it. In his view point there is no religion higher than Truth and Righteousness.[24]

> "A devotee of Truth" says Gandhi, "may not be anything in defence to convention. He must always hold himself

> open to correction and wherever he discovers himself to be wrong, he must confess, it all cost and at one for it.[25]

Gandhi does not give vent to supernaturalism as it does not help to realize the truth as truth. Freedom of religion from dogma gives the largest scope for self expression.[26]

Proofs for the Existence of God

Although Gandhi is not an academician, or a system builder, his study of different religious books especially the *New Testament* and *Bhagavad Gita* and his earnest discussions on matters of religious importance with all kinds of persons prepared him well to stand for the arguments of the existence of God.

There is orderliness in the universe. An unalterable law is governing everything and every being in the universal. According to Gandhi, it is not a blind law as it cannot govern the conduct of living beings. He terms the law that governs all life as God. The blend of cosmological and teleological arguments could be found together.[27]

For Gandhi, God is a mysterious power.

> "There is" says Gandhi, "an indefinable mysterious power that pervades everything. I feel it, though I do not see it. It is this unseen power which makes itself felt and yet defies all proof, because it is so unlike all that I perceive through my senses. It transcends the senses. But is possible to reason out the existence of God to a limited extent".[28]

Gandhi uses the term religion in its broad sense, which implies self-realization or knowledge of the self.[29] He has sought confirmation in the teachings of the great religions especially through the teaching of the *Gita* and learnt that renunciation as the highest form of religion which appealed to him greatly.[30] This indicates to do one's duty without any desire for the result. This central teaching is embodied in the Gita which states: 'Action alone is thine. Leave thou the fruit severely alone. Action is duty, fruit is the right.'[31]

D.M. Datta states:

> "Renunciation for Gandhi was not flying from the world not salvation a post mortem goal. True renunciation is action without selfish motives and true salvation is liberation from the bondage of selfish desires and passions that fetter and torment man".[32]

Diverse Religion

The study of the great religions has helped Gandhi to find that every one of them contained good precepts. He emphasizes that all religions should be regarded equal for all have the same root and the same laws of growth. He is of the opinion that all great religions of the world are true and God given.

> "I believe" says Gandhi, "in the fundamental truth of all great religions of the world. I believe that they are all God given/ and I believe that they were necessary for the people to whom these religions were revealed. And I believe that, if only we could all of us read the scriptures of different faiths from the standpoint of the followers of those faiths, we should find that they were at bottom all one and were all helpful to one another."[33]

Gandhi believes that the diverse religions are the branches of the same tree but they tend to be imperfect as they are interpreted through the imperfect human instrumentality.

Gandhi observes:

> For me the different religions are beautiful flowers from the same garden, or they are branches of the same majestic tree. Therefore they are equally true though being received and interpreted through human instruments equally imperfect.[34]

Although religions are many, they meet at the same point. Gandhi does not subscribe to the fanatic view that there must be one religion. He believes that all religions in essence are one. On the other hand, he strives hard to find common factor to promote religious tolerance.

> "Religions are different roads" says Gandhi, "Converging upon the same point what does it matter that we take different roads, so long as we reach the same goal."[35]

For Gandhi, the root of religion is 'that which binds' while explaining what he means by religion, he states that it is not the Hindu religion which he certainly prizes above all other religions but the religion which transcends Hinduism, which. Changes one's way nature, binds one indissolubly the Truth and ever purifies.[36]

After a long study of religions and experience, Gandhi has arrived at the following conclusions:

He says:

1. that all religions are true.
2. All religions have some error in them all religions are almost as dear to me as my own Hinduism, in as much as all human beings should be as dear to me as one's own close relatives. My own veneration for other faults is the same as that for my own faith; therefore no thought of conversion is possible. The aim of the Fellowship should be to help a Hindu to become a better Hindu, a Musalman to become a better Musalman and a Christian a better Christian.[37]

Gandhi does not believe in the exclude divinity of the *Vedas*. He believes that the *Bible*, the *Koran* and the *Zend Avesta* to be as much divinity inspired as the *Vedas*. He declines to be bound by any interpretation, however learned it may be, if it is repugnant to reason or morality. He tries to understand the spirit of the various scriptures of the world and applies the test of *ahimsa* (non-violence) and Truth laid down by these scriptures for interpretation. He rejects what is consistent with the test of *ahimsa* and appropriates all that is consistent with it.[38]

The study of the *New Testament* especially the *Sermon on the Mount* has produced different impression on him. He compares it with the *Gita*. He says that:

> But I say unto you, that ye resist not evil but who so ever shall smile thee on thy right cheek, turn him the other also. And if any man take away thy coat, let him have the cloak too.[39]

Gandhi was delighted beyond measure by these verses and he tries to unify the teaching of the *Gita*, the light of Asia and the *Sermon on the Mount*.

> "I have" says Gandhi, "not been able to see any difference between the *Sermon on the Mount* and the *Bhagavad Gita*. What the Sermon describes in a graphic manner, the *Bhagavad Gita* reduces to a scientific formula. It say not be a scientific book in the accepted sense of the term, but it has argued out of the law of love - the law of abandon as I would call it - in a scientific manner. The *Sermon on the Mount* gives the same how in wonderful language. The *New Testament* gave me comfort and boundless joy, as it came after the repulsion that parts of the old had given me. Today, supposing I was deprived of the *Gita* and forgot all its contents but had a copy of the Sermon, I should derive the same joy from it as I do from the *Gita*.[40]

Religion and Service

Gandhi is found himself entirely absorbed in the service of the community. The reason behind this is his desire for self-realization. He makes religion, a religion of service as he feels that God could be realized only through service. Service for him is service to the community.[41] Swami

Vivekananda who influenced Gandhi states that service to the poor is service to God.

Gandhi has pointed out:

> I am endeavouring to see God through service of humanity, for I saw that God is neither in Heaven, nor down below, but in veryone. [42]

Gandhi considers man's ultimate aim as the realiza-tion of God. All his political/ social and religious activities have to be guided by the ultimate vision of God. The immediate service of all human beings becomes necessary as the only way to find God is to see Him in His creation and be one with it. This can be realized only through the service of all.

Says Gandhi:

> I am a part and parcel of the whole and I cannot find Him apart from the rest of the humanity. My countrymen are my nearest neighbours. They have become so helpless so resource less so inert that I must concentrate on serving them. If I could persuade myself that I should find Him in Himalayan cave, I would proceed there immediately. But I know that I cannot find Him apart from Humanity.[43]

Religion is not 'ism'. It is not merely intellectual knowledge or belief in any set of doctrines but an innate attribute of the soul. Religion enables us to define our duties in life as a human being and enables us to deal correctly with our fellow beings. We have to know about ourselves. Religion means self-realization or the true nature of the self.[44]

REFERENCES

1. N.K. Devaraja, *Philosophy, Religion and Culture*, p. 206.
2. *Harijan*, 10.2.1940, p. 445.
3. *Young India*, 12.5.1920, p. 2.
4. *Ibid.*, 24.11.1921. p. 365.

5. *Selections from Bose*, P.255.
6. K.M.P. Varma (Ed). *Philosophy of Religion*, p. 71.
7. M.K. Gandhi, *Ethical Religion*, p. 38.
8. *Young India*, 26.9.1929. p. 316.
9. *Harijan*, 6.3.1937. p. 26.
10. *Young India*, 2.3.1922. p. 131.
11. *Ibid.*, 3.9.1925. p. 304
12. *Young India*, 4.12.1924. p. 398.
13. M.K. Gandhi. *My Religion*, p. 4.
14. M.K. Gandhi, *The Story of My Experiments with Truth*, p. 615
15. *Young India*, 4,8.1927. p. 242.
16. *Ibid.*, 11.9.1924. p.
17. Pyarelal, *Mahatma Gandhi - The Last Phase*. 2nd Vol. p. 143.
18. M.K. Gandhi, *The Story of My Experiraents with Truth*, p. V.
19. M.K. Gandhi, *From Yeravda Mandir - Ashram Observances*, p.1.
20. M.K. Gandhi, *The Story of My Experiments with Truth* p. 382
21. *Ibid.*, p.382,
22. *Young India*, 5.3.1925. pp. 80-81.
23. *Ibid.*, 27.8.1925. p. 293.
24. Nirmal Kumar Bose, *Selections from Gandhi*, p. 254.
25. M.K. Gandhi, *The Story of My Experiments with Truth*, p.265.
26. M.K. Gandhi, *Hindu Dharma*. p. 5.
27. D.M. Datta, *The Philosophy of Mahatma Gandhi*, p. 40.
28. *Young India*, 11.10.1928. p. 340.
29. M.K.Gandhi, *The Story of My Experiments with Truth*, p.22
30. *Ibid.*, p. 51.
31. *Young India*, 8.1.1925. p. 16.
32. D.M.Datta, *The Philosophy of Mahatma Gandhi*, p. 44.
33. *Harijan*, 16.2.1934. pp. 5-6.
34. *Ibid.*, 30.1.1937. p. 407.
35. *Hind Swaraj*, p. 50.
36. *Young India*, 12.5.1920. p. 2.

37. N.K. Bose, *Selections from Gandhi*, pp. 258-59.
38. *Young India*, 27.8.1925. p. 293.
39. M.K. Gandhi, *The Story of My Experiments with Truth*, p. 51.
40. *Young India*, 22.12.1927. p. 426.
41. M.K. Gandhi, *The Story of My Experiments with Truth*, p. 118.
42. *Young India*, 4.8.1927. pp. 247-8.
43. *Harijan*, 29.8.1936. p. 226.
44. Pyarelal, *Mahatma Gandhi*. Vol. I. p.

4

Non-Violence

Meaning

Ahimsa literally means non-injury and hence non-killing which is translated as non-violence. It has been used in this sense in the *Upanishads*, Buddhism and Jainism and the orthodox Hindu laws of Manu. But it has been most rigorously interpreted by Jainism which has set the ideal of non-killing or injuring any form of life for any purpose at all.

Non-violence is love without attachment. It is strength without ill-feeling and inaction. It is tolerance without fear and peace without being cowardly. Non-violence is a way of life, devoid of all extremes of passions like anger, enmity, pleasure and pain. All these make up the ideal of ahimsa. *Ahimsa* (non-violence) is never static but ever changing, embracing all aspects of human life.[1]

Gandhi is the pioneer in applying ahimsa for the solution of day to day problems of which the humanity is confronted with. He made it a mission of life to see that ahimsa as the moral means gets its proper place and all the relations and activities are carried on the basis of this universal doctrine. In reality non-violence has become absolute need to the humanity in the modern times.

Gandhian Interpretation of Non-violence

Gandhi interprets non-violence in a new perspective. He redefined the meaning of non-violence. He says, that non-violence is not the crude thing it has been made to appear. Not to hurt any living being is no doubt a part of ahimsa. But it is its least expression. The principle of *himsa* is hurt by every evil thought, by undue haste, by lying, by hatred and by wishing ill to any body.[2]

Gandhi distinguishes between the negative and positive meanings of non-violence:

> "*Ahimsa* is not merely a negative state of harmlessness" says Gandhi, "but it is a positive state of love, of doing good even to the evil-doer. But it does not mean helping the evil-doer to continue the wrong or tolerating it by passive acquiescence. On the contrary, love—the active state of *ahimsa* - requires you to resist the wrong-doer by disassociating yourself from him, even though it may offend him or injure him physically.[3]

Again he says:

> "In its positive form, *ahimsa* means the largest love, the greatest charity".[4]

The Nature of Non-violence

Gandhi describes the nature of non-violence in the following words:

1. "Non-violence is the law of the human race and is infinitely greater than and superior to brute force.
2. In the last resort it does not avail to these who do not possess a living faith in the God of Love.
3. Non-violence affords the fullest protection to one's self-respect and sense of honour, but not always to possession of land or movable property/ through its habitual practice does prove a better bulwark than

the possession of armed men to defend them. Non-violence, in the very nature of things, is of no assistance in the defense of ill-gotten gains and immoral acts.

4. Individuals or nations who would practice non-violence must be prepared to sacrifice their all except honour. It is, therefore, inconsistent with the possession of other people's countries, i.e., modern imperialism, which is frankly based on force for its defiance.
5. Non-violence is a power which can be wielded equally by all - children, youngmen and women or grown-up people, provided they have a living faith in the God of Love and have therefore, equal love for all mankind. When non-violence is accepted as the law of life, it must pervade the whole being and not to be applied to isolated acts.
6. It is erroneous to suppose that while the law is good enough for individuals, it is not for the masses of mankind. The practice of non-violence is more than the daily food. Non-violence which is the spiritual food, has to be taken continually.[5]

The Law of Our Existence

Gandhi holds the view that man has steadily been progressing towards non-violence. He refers to the history of mankind and finds the remote anscestors as cannibals and violent. In the next stage man has become a hunter. Being ashamed of his violent life as hunter, he disowned hunting. He started relying principally on earth for agriculture to make his iving. He became civilized, founded villages and towns. He became a member of a family, a community and a nation. All these stages of Man's life indicate the progressing non-violence and diminishing violence. Had man been violent/

the human species would have become extinct by this time/ says Gandhi. Non-violence is the law of the species.[6]

The religion of non-violence is not meant merely for the rashes and saints. It is also meant for the common peoples, says Gandhi. Non-violence is the law of the species as violence is the law of brute. The spirit lies dormant in the brute. He knows no law than that of physical might. The dignity of man requires obedience to a higher law. The rashes who discovered the law of non-violence in the midst of violence are greater geniuses than Newton. They are themselves greater warriors than Wellington. Having known the use of arms, they realized their uselessness. They taught a weary world that its salvation lay not through violence but through non-violence.[7]

Non-violence as Creed and Policy

Adoption of non-violence as a mere policy is distinct from adoption of non-violence as creed. While adoption of non-violence as a mere policy remains as a plan of action depending on the human situation and expediency. The policy is given up if it is not proved to be congercal and useful whereas adoption of non-violence as creed is based on the firm conviction and belief. The person who adopts it does not fail.

Any one who advocates the adoption of non-violence as a mere matter of policy is likely to break down at the critical juncture.[8] So there is need for those who advocate non-violence to live a life of non-violence without resisting evil with evil.[9]

Gandhi has made a clear cut distinction between non-violence as a creed and non-violence as a policy and between the non-violence of the strong and the non-violence of the weak.[10]

Gandhi is convinced out of his experience that permanent good can never be the outcome of untruth and violence. For him non-violence is an unchangeable creed and it has to be pursued in the face of violence raging around.

> "Non-violence" says Gandhi, "with a non-violent man is no merit. In fact it becomes difficult to say whether it is non-violence at all. But when it is pitted against violence, then one realizes the difference between the two. This we cannot do unless we are ever wakeful, ever vigilant, ever striving.[11]

Non-violence is lawful but violence can never be awful. Violence is not lawful not according to the man-made law but according to the law—made by Nature of man.[12]

Gandhi considers non-violence as a creed for it is breath of his life. He has laid down five simple actions of this creed:

1. Non-violence implies a complete self-purification which is within the human reach which means rigorous ethical discipline and the taking of vows.

2. Man for man, the strength of non-violence is in exact proportion to the ability but not to the will of the non-violent person to inflict violence which implies that a government which renounces nuclear weapons is potentially though not automatically capable of displaying *ahimsa* to an enormous extent.

3. Non-violence is superior to violence without any exception, i.e., that the power a at the disposal of a non-violent person is always greater than had he been violent which presupposes the idea that power is not merely independent of force but that greater the power of a moral or political authority, the less the force needed for the exercise of that authority.

4. This action implies that there is no such thing as defeat in-non-violence and the end of violence is surest defeat which implies that non-violence be

explained in terms of the moral inadequacy of the user, and similarly violence seems to succeed only if we take too narrow or short-sighted view of success.

5. The ultimate end of non-violence is surest victory it such term is used of non-violence. In reality, there is no sense of defeat when there is no sense of victory which implies that the victory of non-violence never does aim at defeating anyone but merely aims at achieving a desirable result.[13]

Ahimsa as represented by Gandhi stands as an ideal to be reached. As he realized that most of the people can not become absolutists with regard to ahimsa, he therefore recommended the relevance and responsibleness of ahimsa as a policy as the next best thing to non-violence as a creed rather than to express it as a mere rationalization of physical weakness or an expression of mere expediency.[14]

Non-violence and Truth

Gandhi says that truth and non-violence are as old as hills. He is a ceaseless seeker of truth and he describes his life as a series of 'Experiments with Truth'. The inseparable nexus between truth and non-violence could be traced in his teachings. He holds that truth can be experienced through non-violent means. For him non-violence is the best and easiest way to realize truth.

Gandhi insisted on truth and non-violence in every field of human activity. According to Gandhi, it is not possible to seek or find truth without non-violence:

> "Without *ahimsa*" says Gandhi, "it is not possible to seek and find Truth. *Ahimsa* and Truth are so intertwined that it is practically impossible to disentangle and separate them. They are like the two sides of a coin, or rather of a smooth, unstamped metallic disc. Who can say which is the observe and which is -the reverse.[15]

> Nevertheless *ahimsa* is the means; Truth is the end. Means to be means must always be within our reach, and so *ahimsa* is our supreme duty. If we take care of the means, we are bound to reach the end sooner or later.[16]

Non-violence is not the goal, but truth is the goal. The ultimate goal of life to Gandhi is absolute truth which is knowable to man through partial truth. A higher law of duty has required man to seek the final truth fearlessly, actively and selflessly. Non-violence is the superior ethic which enable roan to live a good life but it is not the goal in itself:[17]

> "Ahimsa is not the goal" says Gandhi. "Truth is the goal. But we have no means of realizing truth in human relationships except through the practice of *ahimsa*. A stead fast pursuit of *ahimsa* is inevitably bound to truth—not so violence. That is why I swear by *ahimsa*.[18]

Gandhi says that truth without non-violence is not truth but untruth.[19] Violence cannot take us to the goal as it has its roots in anger, selfishness, lust etc. Violence attacks not only the sin and the evil but also the sinner and the evil doer which is offending and stands against the great truth. Had untruth endeared and nothing were true to itself and to others and if all laws of life and nature were uncertain and undependable, the universe would have turned into chaos.[20]

According to Gandhi, truth which is the object of our quest, is not outside ourselves, but within us. The more we rely on violence in dealing with those who create difficulties, the more we recede from truth.[21] *Ahimsa* divorced from truth would be demoralizing instead of liberating.[22]

Although Gandhi in practice has laid more stress on non-violence rether than on truth, he maintains that truth is superior to non-violence. He says that truth and non-violence are convertible terms, but he does not hesitate to leave non-violence to abide by the truth which "is supreme if the situation demands.

Non-violence and Cowardice

Gandhi has expected people to be fearless but not to be weak and cowardly. He considers weakness, cowardice and fear as sins against the human spirit for a person in the grip of fear is capable of committing any crime however heinous it might be.[23] The practice of non-violence makes the people brave and fearless. A violent soldier despite courage and brevity he has may have fear in his heart. Non-violence can only be exercised by the Truly brave who have cast off all their fear and fearlessness can be experienced through non-violence than through violence.[24]

Gandhi preferred violence to cowardice. He believed that non-violence is infinitely superior to violence.

> "I do believe" says Gandhi, "that where there is any choice between cowardice and violence, I would advise violence. But I believe that non-violence is infinitely superior to violence, forgiveness is more manly than punishment. Forgiveness adorns a soldier".[25]

He believes that there is hope for violent man to be some day non-violent, but there is no such scope for the coward to be non-violent. The non-violence as visualized by Gandhi is of different type than what it appears to be for it does not remain static but tends to be dynamic depending on human situation. He says that his non-violence fully accommodates violence. If people do not know how to depend themselves, the women by non-violence, they must at least be able defend all these even by violence. Non-violence is not a cover for cowardice. It is a supreme virtue of the brave. Non-violence pre-supposes brevity. Exercise of non-violence requires for greater bravery than that of swordranship. Cowardice is completely inconsistent with non-violence.[26]

> "Non-violence and cowardice are contradictory terms" says Gandhi, "Non-violence is the greatest virtue, cowardice is the greatest vice. Non-violence springs

> from love. Cowardice from hate. Non-violence always suffers; cowardice would always inflict suffering".[27]

If a person who is faced with danger behaves like a mouse, he is called rightly a coward. He harbors violence and hatred in his heart. He would kill his enemy if he could without hurting himself. He is a stranger to non-violence.[28] Even if a person is weak in body, if it is a shame to flee, he will stand his ground and die at his post. This would be non-violence and bravery. Despite weakness, if a person will use the strength he has in inflicting injury to his opponent, and die in the attempt, this is bravery but not non-violence when his duty is face danger, but if he feels it is cowardice. In this case, the man will have love or charity in him but the second and cases, there would be dislike or distrust and fear.[29]

The Power of Non-violence

Non-violence alone continue to be the highest good of mankind, not merely in the next world but in this world also. Gandhi objects to violence because when it appears to do well, the good is only temporary. But the evil it does is permanent.[30] In the opinion of Gandhi non-violence is the greatest force mightier than the mightiest weapons of destruction:

> "Non-violence is the greatest force" says Gandhi, "at the disposal of mankind. It is mightier than the mightiest weapon of destruction devised by the ingenuity of man. Destruction is not the law of the humans".[31]

Gandhi has applied non-violence in every walk of his life, i.e., domestic, institution, economic and political, but he does not know of even a single instance in which it has faceted. Where non-violence has seemed to have failed, he has ascribed it to his imperfections. In his passionate search for truth, he discovered non-violence. He could find several possibilities in non-violence.[32]

> "Non-violence" says Gandhi, "in its dynamic condition means conscious suffering. It does not mean meek submission to the will of the evil doer but it means the pitting of ones whole soul against the will of the tyrant, working under this law of our being, it is possible for a single individual to defy the whole might of an unjust empire to save his honour, his soul and lay the foundation for that empire's fall or its regeneration".[33]

An armed soldier relies on his weapons for strength. He becomes generally helpless if his weapons are taken away. But in the case of a person who has truly realized the principle of non-violence, he has the God-given strength and nothing would match it.[34] Gandhi considers *ahimsa* (non-violence) as a science. There is no place for the word failure in the vocabulary of science.[35]

> "Non-violence is like radium in action" says Gandhi, "an infinitesimal quantity of it embedded in a malignant growth, acts continuously, silently and ceaselessly it has transformed the whole mass of the diseased tissue" into a healthy one. Similarly, even a little of true non-violence acts in a silent, subtle, unseen way and leavens the whole society".[36]

Violence can effectively be met by non-violence. This is an old established truth. The weapon of violence even if it is the atom bomb becomes useless when matched against true non-violence. It requires a lot of understanding and strength of mind. It is different from what is needed in military schools and colleges.[37]

The precept 'hate the sin but not the sinner' is rarely practised. As a result hatred spreads all over the world.[38]

Practice of Non-violence

Gandhi lays more stress on the practice of non-violence. He considers non-violence as the greatest force at the disposal of mankind. The use of non-violence is not restricted to individuals alone but it can be practiced on mass scale also.

The practice of non-violence proceeds with the basic principle "that what holds good in respect of one self equally applies to the whole universe. All mankind in essence are alike. What is possible for one person is possible for everybody".[39]

Gandhi holds that if one does not practise non-violence in one's personal relations with others and hopes to use it in bigger affairs, one is vastly mistaken. Non-violence like charity must begin at home.[40]

> "Non-violence is not a cloistered virtue" says Gandhi, "confined only to the Rishi and the cave-dweller. It is capable of being practised by the millions, not with full knowledge of its implications, but because it is the Law of our species. It distinguishes man from the brute. But man has not shed the brute in him. He has to strive to do so. This striving applies to the practice of non-violence".[41]

Contemporary Non-violent Resistance

There is need to examine how Gandhian Ideas have been received in other countries of the world and how they are taking shape of social action in a new way which suffer from dissociation against the existing order based on violence and mass destruction. There are challenges faced by the Gandhian thought theoretically and practically. There is need to give a context and a strong voice to the challenges and examine how they are thoroughly tested.

After the invention of atomic power, rethinking to a greater extent has begun about military affairs all over the world. While some countries are busily engaged in the proliferation of the atomic weapons, some have vehemently protested against this in a non-violent manner.

History teaches that no durable solution could be found except by persuasion and common consent to solve any human problem.[42]

Gandhi fought for the most fundamental battle of human rights which can be termed as the right to life through non-violent resistance. He has become more relevant than when he was alive. Although the Gandhian thought has suffered a callous neglect in the country where he was born, Martin Luther King in U.S.A. inspired lakhs of people to rise against the Martial Law regime in a non-violent manner. Quite recently and vividly in USSR Sukhorov fasted for the reunion of his daughter with her husband and Mother. Theresa served the wounded and afflicted in the war torn Lebanon, are on the non-violent path of Gandhi.[43]

Martin Luther King conducted the non-violent resistance movement against the colour discrimination in USA. His object was not only to resist apartheid but also to convert rest of his country men the whites into the recognition of the dignity and equality of the coloured people.[44]

It is because of the non-violent methods of his protests and the scope and depth of his active moral concern, Martin Luther King Jr. occupies a unique position in history of the creative dissent in the United State.[45]

While Martin Luther King was at more houses, he was deeply influenced by the writings of Henry David Thoreau on Civil Disobedience. At crozer seminary in Pennsylvania, King studied the books of the great theologians and philosophers in search of finding possible solutions to racial inequality. He emerged from these readings much more enlightened about religion which could play a positive role in social change. He gained a great knowledge of the historical and structural nature of human societies.[46]

Martin Luther King was greatly influenced by the teachings of Mahatma Gandhi. He later adopted his non-violent doctrine as the most effective weapon against racial segregation in USA. One Sunday afternoon, King travelled to Philadelphia to hear a sermon by Dr. Mordecai Johnson who spoke on the life and teachings of Mahatma Gandhi. His message had an immediate and profound impact upon Martin Luther King. While reading the work of Gandhi, King lost his skepticism of the power of love and began appreciating its usefulness and potency in the area of social reform.[47]

The Gandhian technique of love and non-violence gave Martin Luther King a potent instrument for social and collective transformation. Blacks could be taught this to use in their struggle against oppression and injustice.[48] King viewed violence as immoral. It could achieve success but the success is temporary at best.[49]

For King non-violence is both constructive and its cleansing aspect is the instrument of social progress. When non-violence tends to be constructive, it develops the moral strength of the people and disciplines them for the use of non-violent direct action.[50]

Martin Luther King explains his philosophy in the following words:

> "I believe in a militant, non-violent approach in which the individual stands up against an unjust system, using sit-ins, legal action boycotts, votes and everything else except violence or hate".[51]

The King's philosophy of non-violence was a synthesis of the teachings of Jesus Christ and Mahatma Gandhi. The *Sermon on the Mount* provided the motivating ideal of love. Gandhi provided the method of mass non-violent direct action. The love advocated by Jesus was expressed by the Greek word 'agape' which was defined as unconditional, disinterested goodwill towards all men and aims to preserve and community at the same time.[52]

In the Montgomery bus boycott and in all other crusades for social justice, Martin Luther King instructed his followers about the necessity of love for all men (*agape*). He explained the Montgomery bus boycott programme in the following words:

> This is a protest of passive resistance depending upon moral and spiritual forces. We will return good for evil. Christ showed us the way and Mahatma Gandhi showed as it could work.[53]

The Montgomery bus boycott launched by King, virtually brought him into a position of national and international prominence and made his emergence as a symbol of racial justice.[54] After the boycott, King's devotion to Gandhi's non-violent method increased.[55]

While explaining the main characteristics or the non-violent resistance in the Montgomery boycott, King like Gandhi emphasized that his resistance was directed against the forces of evil than against the persons who do the evil. He often proclaimed that non-violent resistance does not aim to humiliate or defeat the opponents but aims to liberate them from their prejudice and fear. He asserted that segregationists had been taught wrong. They themselves were victimized by the evil system they perpetuated segregation has given some whites a false sense of superiority and deprived them of genuine humility, honesty and love.[56]

King and the civil rights movements had an effective technique to force Kennedy and later Johnson, in the right direction – the use of massive street demonstrations and protests. The world observed via radio, the mass media and television. The momentous mass confrontations in Birmingham in 1963 and Selma in 1965 are outstanding examples of this strategy of action.[57]

Like Gregg and Gandhi, King stressed that it is better to suffer evil than to inflect it. King contended that instead of multiplying violence and bitterness, the non-violent resister by his willingness to suffer may arouse a sense of shame in the opponent and thereby bring about a transformation and change of heart.[58]

The Struggle is My Life wrote Nelson Mandela, in a letter from the underground. Under his leadership, the African National Congress (ANC) has followed the policy of non-violence in the struggle against the South African government for freedom and justice.

Nelson Mandela adopt a more militant progamme of new forms of mass action by strikes, boycotts and civil disobedience against the repressive legislation. The ANC working with the Indian Congress and father Olives organized the Difiance Campaign directed against specific unjust laws of apartheid.[59]

Mandela fought for the equal political rights of the people. About his dedication to the struggle he quietly spoke:

> I have cherished the ideal of a democratic and free society in which all persons live together in harmony and with equal opportunities. It is an ideal which it needs be, it is an ideal for which I am prepared to die.[60]

REFERENCES

1. Kotturam George, *Ahimsa – Gautama to Gandhi*, p. 6.
2. M.K. Gandhi, *From Yeravda Mandir - Ashram Observances*, p. 7.
3. *Young India*. 25.8.1920. p. 2.
4. *Speeches and Writings of Mahatma Gandhi*, p. 346,
5. *Harijan*, 5.9.1936. p. 236.
6. *Ibid.*, 11.8.1940. p. 245.
7. *Young India*, 11.8.1920. p. 3.
8. M.K. Gandhi, *Non-violence in Peace and War*, Vol. I, p. 505
9. *Ibid.*, p. 506.
10. Raghavan Iyer, *Moral and Political Thought of Mahatma Gandhi*, p. 192.
11. *Harijan*, 2.4.1938. p. 64.
12. *Ibid.*, 27.10.1946. p. 369,
13. Raghavan Iyer, *op.cit.*, pp.193-94.
14. *Ibid.*, p. 196.
15. *Gandhi Marg Quarterly*, Gandhi Peace Foundation, July 1975, p.199.

16. M.K. Gandhi, *From Yeravda Mandir*, pp. 12-13
17. Paul F. Power, *Gandhi on World Affairs*, p. 127.
18. *Harijan*, 23.6.1946. p. 199.
19. *Young India*, p. 1295.
20. Gopinath Dhavan, *The Political Philosophy of Mahatma Gandhi*, pp. 60-61.
21. M.K. Gandhi, *From Yeravda Mandir*, p.10.
22. Gopinath Dhavan, *The Political Philosophy of Mahatma Gandhi*, p. 60.
23. J.B. Kripalani, *Gandhian Thought*, p. 143.
24. *Ibid.*, p. 188
25. *Young India*, 11.8.1920. p. 3
26. *Ibid.*, 12.8.19 26. p. 285
27. *Ibid.*, 31.10.1929. p. 356, *Harljan*, 20.7.1935. pp. 180-1
29. *Harijan*, 17.8.1935. p. 111
30. *Young India*, 21.5.19 25. p. 178.
31. *Harijan*, 20.7.1935. p. 10.
32. *Ibid.*, 6.7.1940. p. 185.
33. *Young India*. 1.8.19 20. p. 3
34. *Harijan*, 19.11.1938. pp. 341-2.
35. *Ibid.*, 6.5.1939. p. 113.
36. *Ibid.*, 12.11.1938. p. 327.
37. *Ibid.*, 1.6.1947. p. 172.
38. M.K. Gandhi, *The Story of My Experiments with Truth*, p 203.
39. *Harijan*, 12.11.1938. p. 327.
40. *Ibid.*, 28.1.1939. p. 441.
41. *Ibid.*, 4.11.1939. 331.
42. S.R. Bakshi, *Gandhi and Ideology of Non-Violence*, p. 111. Ramjee Sing, *Relevance of Gandhian Thought*, p. vii.
44. Nirmal Kumar Bose, *Gandhism and Modern India*, p. 114.
45. John J. Ausbro, Martin Luther King JR. *The Making of a Mind*. p. XIII.
46. Peter J. Albert, *We Shall Over Come*, p. 57.
47. Hames Walton J.R, *The Political Philosophy of Martin Luther King JR*. p. 42.

48. *op.cit.*, p. 43
49. *Ibid.*, p. 59.
50. *Ibid.*, p. 107.
51. Nisssim Ezekiel, *A Martin King Reader*, p. V.
52. James A. Colaiaco, *Martin Luther King Jr. An Apostle of Militant Non-violence*. p. 24.
53. Nissim Ezekiel, *A Martin King Reader*, p. VI.
54. James A. Colaiaco, *Martin Luther King Jr. An Apostle of Militant Non-violence*, p. 19.
55. *Ibid.*, p. 25.
56. *Ibid.*, p.137.
57. Peter J. Albert, *We Shall Overcome*, p. 55.
58. John J. Ansbro, *Martin Luther King Jr., The Making of a Mind*. p.150.
59. Nelson Mandela, *Struggle is My Life*, p. 2.
60. *Ibid.*, p. 2.

5

Sarvodaya

Sarvodaya literally means the uplift of all and welfare of all. *Sarvodaya* is a social concept for it lays emphasis on society and its development. Mahatma Gandhi considers the human life as a synthetic whole which cannot be divided into Water-tight compartments, moral, political, economic, social, environmental and collective. They are interconnected.

It appears that Mahatma Gandhi borrowed the concept *Sarvodaya* from Samantabhadra. As early as 2nd century A.D. Samantabhadra, the Jaina commentator used the word to indicate the all embracing character of Jainism.

Gandhi used this word *Sarvodaya* in his autobiography and gave Gujarati translation of Ruskin's "Unto This Last' the title *Sarvodaya*. It exerted profound influence on Gandhi and brought about an instantaneous transformation in his life. Ruskin's writings are found to be very much serviceable to the humanity. He gave a stable definition of wealth and suggested ways and means of acquiring wealth under certain moral conditions that govern the society. In the writings of John Ruskin more stress was laid for the attainment of honesty and the moral values. Ruskin expressed the view that there is no difference of honour and human dignity for the wages of labourers, a middle class man and a man from the higher rank.[1]

They are:

(a) That the good of the individual is contained in the good of all.

(b) That a labourer's work has the same values as the barber's inasmuch as all have the same right of earning their livelihood for their work.

(c) That a life of a labour, i.e., the life of the tiller of the the soil and the handicraftsman, is the life worth living. [2]

Mahatma Gandhi resolved to apply those principles into practice. *Sarvodaya* stands as a solution to the social, political and economic problems. *Sarvodaya* is a humanistic idealistic is mainly connected with the development of the society in which man is a part and parcel. *Sarvodaya* ideology is considered to be a creative blend of all humanistic and altruistic tendencies which can be interpreted in terms of an integrated social philosophy in this age of crisis. It seeks to redeem and reform the individual and society.[3] *Sarvodaya* makes man to be conscious of his responsibilities and helps to establish an order in the society. The principles of *Sarvodaya* are consistent with non-violence.

Dada Dharmadhikari seeks to highlight the distinction between Sarvodaya and the westernisms. He speaks of three stages in the evolution of human thought. First came Darwin who advocated the principle of the 'survival of the Fittest". Next came the doctrine 'Live and Let live'. *Sarvodaya* does a step further and asserts "Live in order to help others live".[4]

Sarvodaya and Utilitarianism

Sarvodaya concept does not subscribe to the utilitarian formula the greatest good to the greatest number but will strive for the greatest of all. The follower of Sarvodaya will therefore will be willing to die so that others may live. He serves himself with the rest by himself dying. The greatest good of all inevitably includes the utilitarian formula the greatest good to the greatest number. Therefore, he and the utilitarian converge in many points in their career. But when the time comes, they must part company and even work in opposite directions. The utilitarian will never sacrifice if the situation demands whereas the absolutist will even sacrifice himself.[5]

Sarvodaya while at the all-round development and well-being of man seeks to build a new society on the foundations of the traditionally accepted spiritual and moral values and attempts to meet the challenge of the contemporary world.[6] It attempts achieve the life good of equality, unity, fraternity and other values of life. Sarvodaya helps to avoid social, economic and political exploitation for the good of all. There will be no place for tyranny, violence, and exploitation when non-violent action is involved. Sarvodaya stands against the principle of a few enjoying at the cost of many.

Unity of Man

Sarvodaya the greatest good of all as Gandhi puts it is the outcome of his spiritual outlook in life. While asserting that his approach to the human life is spiritual he wrote:

> I believe in *Advaita*. I believe in the essential unity of man and for that matter, of all that lives. Therefore, I believe that if one man gains spiritually, the whole world gains with him and if one man falls, the whole world falls to that extent.[7]

The spiritual law does not work in its own field. On the contrary it expresses itself through the ordinary activities of life affecting the economic, the social and the political fields. Gandhi had faith on man and his abilities. Man is capable of transforming the whole world as the world of human welfare.

Identity and Service of the Poor

Gandhi could not imagine anything nobler or more national than to do the labour that the poor must do and thus identify ourselves with the poor and through them with all mankind. For Gandhi the better worship of God than to labour for the poor.[8]

Gandhi holds that all the activities of man have to be centred in truth for truth is the breath of our life. The moment the stage in the pilgrims progress is reached, all other rules of correct living would follow without any effort. He maintains "But without Truth it is impossible to observe any principle or rule of life".[9]

Gandhi held that man's ultimate aim is the realization of God and all his activities, social, political and religious have to be guided by the ultimate aim of the vision of God. He pointed out that the immediate service of all human beings is the absolute need to realize God.

> "The immediate service of all human beings" says Gandhi, "becomes a necessary part of the Endeavour simply because the only way to find God is to see Him in His creation and be one with it. This can only be done by the service of all. I am part and parcel of the whole land I cannot find Him apart from the rest of the humanity. My countrymen are my nearest neighbours. They have become so helpless, so resource-less so inert that I must concentrate myself on serving them".[10]

Gandhi held that God myriad-formed. He could find Him sometimes in the spinning-wheel, at times in Communal unity and then again in removal of untouchability.[11]

Charkha as Comforter

Gandhi maintained that he who spins before the poor and invite the poor to do likewise, serves God as no one less does. For Gandhi, the spinning is the greatest prayer, the greatest worship and the greatest sacrifice.[12]

The world is weary of the after-effects of the war said Gandhi. He held the view that even as the Charkha is India comforter today, it may be world's tomorrow, because it stands, not for the greatest good of the great number, but for the greatest good of all. [13] Gandhi in this connection referred to the Ruskin's book '*Unto This Last*' which brought about a change in his life. We must do *Unto This Last* said Gandhi. All must be given equal opportunity. If everybody is given the equal opportunity, every human being has the same possibility for spiritual growth. The spinning wheel symbolizes this.[14]

Self-purificaton

Gandhi attached great importance to self-purification. Without self-purification one cannot identify himself without anything that lives and the observance of the law of *ahimsa* (non-violence) remains an empty dream. God can never be realized without the pure heart. So self-purification means, purification in all walks of life. Purification being highly infectious, purification of oneself necessarily leads to the purification of ones surroundings. To attain perfect purity one has to become absolutely passion free in thought, speech and deed and to rise above the opposing currents of love and hatred, attachment and repulsion.[15]

Duties and Rights

According to Gandhi the true source of rights is duty. If one discharges his duties, it will not be difficult and far to seek rights. Without discharging one's duties, if one runs after the rights, they will escape like a will-o-the-wisp. The more one perserves them, the farther they will fly.

Gandhi referred to the Krishna's words in which the same teaching is embodied.

> Action alone is thine. Leave thou the fruit severely alone. Action is duty; fruit is the right.[16]

Right action automatically to him who duly performs his duties. He says, "In fact, the right to perform one's duties is the only right that is worth living for and dying for. It covers all legitimate rights, all the rest is grab under one guise or another and contains in it seeds of *himsa*".[17] He holds that if everyone instead of insisting on rights, does his duty, the rule of order will be established immediately among the making. He suggested that rights that do not flow directly from duty well performed are not worth having for there will be usurpations. It would be better if they are discarded. A wretched parent who claims obedience from his children without discharging his duty excites nothing but contempt by them.[18]

Yagna

Gandhi holds that *yagna* means an act directed to the welfare of others which is done without expecting any return from it. The *Gita* teaches and experience testifies that all actions that cannot come under the category of *yagna* promotes bondage.

The world subsists because of *yagna* and cannot subsist even for a single moment without it. In the *Gita* it has been stated that *yagna* came with the creation itself. The body which we have has been given to us only in order that we may serve all creation with it. Therefore the *Gita* says that he who eats without offering *yagna* eats stolen food so every single act of one who leads a pure life should be in the nature of *yagna*. Consciously or unconsciously, everyone renders some service or the other. If the habit of doing this service is cultivated deliberately, the desire for service will steadily grow stronger. This would not only make a few happy but that of the whole world at large.[19]

Yagna is duty to be performed or service to be rendered throughout the 24 hours of the day. Gandhi held the view that by serving without any desire, means not to favour others, but overselves even as in discarding a debt, we serve only ourselves, lighten our burden and fulfil our duty. All are bound to place their resources at the disposal of humanity. If such be the law, indulgence ceases to hold a place in life and gives way to renunciation.

By renunciation, Gandhi meant not abandoning the world and retiring into the forest. The spirit of renunciation should rule all the activities of the human life. If the spirit of renunciation rules, a merchant who operates in the sacrificial spirit, will have crores passing through his hands, but he will use his abilities for service. He does not cheat or speculate but will lead a simple lie. He will not injure a living soul and will lose millions rather than harm anybody.

Gandhi pointed out:

> A life of sacrifice is the pinnacle of art, and is full of true joy. *Yagna* is not *yagna* it one feels it be burdensome or annoying self-indulgence leads to destruction and renunciation to immortality. Joy has no independent existence. It depends upon our attitude of life.[20]

Gandhi said that one who would serve will not waste a thought upon his own comforts. He would take only what he strictly needs leaving the rest. He will be calm and free from anger. When one takes precedence over service of self, it is voluntary service.[21]

Socialism

Socialism is a science which visualizes a new society and a new civilization based upon modern scientific knowledge. The socialists are marked by the two fundamental beliefs. The first fundamental belief is that the existing system of society and its institution should be condemned as unjust and morally unsound. The second fundamental belief of socialism is that there can be created different forms of society with different institutions, based upon moral values which would tend to improve. The existing system of society is morally unsound as there is much injustice that one would revolt against it. The conditions governing the society produce a few rich and many poor wherein the few are permitted to lead a life of luxury whereas millions are denied the bare needs and minimum wants of life.[22]

In the words of Emile Durkheim, socialism is entirely oriented towards the future which is a plan for the reconstruction of societies, a programme for a collective life which does not exist yet or in the way it is dreamed of. It is an ideal. [23] Socialism consists of narrow subordination of the individual to the collective. It is a tendency which demands the subordination of the individual to the collective. It is a tendency which demands the subordination of individual welfare to the welfare of the community.[24]

Sarvodaya stands for the emancipation of the people and tends to elevate all the people to a level of human dignity and equality. *Sarvodaya* aims at the welfare of all and asserts that the good of the people is contained in the good of all the whole of the humanity. It aims at the economic, social and political equality to establish the order and makes the way to provide equal opportunities all sections of the people. The ideal of *Sarvodaya* plan sets out to achieve a non-violent, non-exploitative, cooperative society which shall not be based on caste or class and in which there will be equal opportunity for all. The present competitive economy shall be replaced by a social economy which is based on cooperation.[25]

Mahatma Gandhi lays more stress on the values of individual and social life that socialism strives to achieve and make the bases of a new civilization.

"Real socialism" says Gandhi, has been handed down to us by our ancestors who taught 'All land belongs to Gopal, where there is the boundary line? Man is the maker of that line and he can therefore un make it. Gopal literally means shepherd, it also means God. In modern language it means the State i.e. the people. That the land today does not belong to the people is too true. But the fault is not in the teaching. It is in us who have not lived up to it.[26] Gandhi wanted that every one should have right over the land and the land should not be in the hands of the select few was this type of system makes the poor still poorer and the richer still richer.

> "Socialism is a beautiful word", says Gandhi, "and so far as I am aware, in socialism, all the members of society are equal – none low, none high. In the individual body, the head is not high because it is the top of the body, nor are the soles of the feet low because they touch the earth. Even as members of the individual body are equal so are the members of society. This is socialism".[27]

In socialism, stress is laid on the material and vital perfection attained through the devise of socio-economic structure. Sarvodaya does not neglate the political and economic satisfactions and requirements. Sarvodaya on the other hand does not stand against the importance of material commodities. It does not regard them as the only goal of human endeavour but looks for and for the higher values of life as the goal. Sarvodaya is not confined to the mere theory of ethical justice only but also emphasizes for social, economic and political justice. [28] Sarvodaya is radical and revolutionary in character.

V.P. Varma holds that socialism and sarvodaya are kindred philosophies in two respects. They derive their profound moral appeal from the rootedness of the fundamental belief in the good of the whole community in the place of the narrow pursuit of the oligarchical minority of plutocrats. Both stress that there should be a social appropriation and equitable distribution of the goods of society.[29]

Although some fundamental similarities between socialism and Sarvodaya could be noticed, the means and methods adopted are different. In socialism, society has got control over the individual. The rules and regulations of the state are imperative and the individuals have to follow them very strictly. If the situation demands, violence is also justified in the socialist type of government to achieve the goal.

V.P. Varma observes that there are two short in the socialist philosophy. The basic technique for effectuating socialism is supposed to be nationalization. But the possibility of entrenching the control of the bureaucrats is not ruled out. This may be called another name for state capitalism. From the standpoint of Sarvodaya the socialist belief in positive state action as the sovereign remedy for human ills is unfounded. Sarvodaya aims at the withering of the state and feels that steps should be taken to minimized the functions of the state and its control over the individual. The functions of the state can be minimized provided there is decentralization of powers. So Sarvodya pleads for villagization. In an agrarian society, collectivization has to be enforced by the coercive measures fo totalitarianism as the farmers will not willingly part with the ownership of land. So Sarvodaya pleads for the ownership by the village community. While socialism believes in nationalization, Sarvodaya accepts village ownership. Socialism adheres in certain cases to the concept of violent revolution but Sarvodaya has no place for violence.[30]

Socialism does not equate or distribute its power. So the question of decentralization of power does not arise but Sarvodaya aims a decentralized economy and political power. When the economic decentralization is made operative by making the production labour intensive instead of capital intensive, it contributes to the welfare of all.

Jayaprakash Narayan holds that the merging of socialism with Sarvodya becomes possible when socialism tends to give up the exercise of violence and concentration of power.

REFERENCES

1. John Ruskin, *Unto This Last*, pp. 12-17.
2. M.K. Gandhi, *The Story of My Experiments with Truth*, p. 124.
3. V. Narayana Karan Reddy, *Sarvodaya Ideology and Acharaya Vinoba*, p. 1.
4. Adi Doctor, *Sarvodaya: A Political and Economic Study*, p. 4.
5. *Young India*, 9-12-1926, p. 432.
6. V.P. Varma, *The Political Philosophy of Mahatma Gandhi and Sarvodaya*, p.329.
7. *Young India*, 4-12-1824, p. 398.
8. *Ibid*, 20-12-1928, p. 420.
9. M.K. Gandhi, *From Yeravada Mandir*, p. 2.
10. *Harijan 29-8-1936*, p. 226.
11. *Ibid*, 8-5-1937, p. 93.
12. *Young India*, 24-9-1925, p. 331.
13. *Ibid*, 10-2-1927, p. 43.
14. *Harijan*, 17-11-1946, p. 404.
15. M.K. Gandhi, *The Story of My Experiments with Truth*, p. 371.
16. *Young India*, 8-1-1925, p. 15.
17. *Harijan*, 29-5-1939, p. 143.
18. *Ibid*, 6-7-1947, p. 217.
19. M.K. Gandhi, *From Yeravada Mandir*, pp. 53-54.
20. *Ibid*, p. 56.
21. *Ibid*, p. 57.
22. Asok Mehata, *Democratic Socialism*, p. 63.
23. Emile Durkheim, *Socialism and Saint Simen*. p. 5.
24. *Ibid*, p. 4.
25. Jayaprakash Narayan, *Socialism – Sarvodaya and Democracy*, p. 92.

26. *Harijan,* 2-1-1937, p.375.
27. *Ibid,* 13-7-1947, p.232.
28. Vinoba Bhave, *Bhudan Ganga,* Vol. I, p. 251.
29. V.P. Varma, *op.cit.*, p. 336.
30. *Ibid*, p. 337.

6

Satyagraha

Meaning of *Satyagraha*

The word 'satyagraha' is of Sanskrit origin which literally means holding on to Truth. It means therefore truth force. It is also known as soul-force as truth is soul or spirit. *Satyagraha* excludes the use of violence because man is not capable of knowing the absolute truth therefore he is not competent to punish. The word *'satyagraha'* was coined in South Africa to distinguish the non-violent resistance of the South Africa from the contemporary passive resistance, of the suffragetts and others but it is not conceived as a weapon of the weak.[1]

The word *'satyagraha'* was coined by Mahatma Gandhi in South Africa. He also called it love-force. He discovered in the earliest stages that pursuit of truth did not admit of violence being inflicted on one's opponent but he must be weaned from error by patience and sympathy what appear to be truth to one person may appear to be error to the other person. The doctrine came to mean vindication of truth not by inflicting suffering on the opponent but on one's own self.[2]

Passive Resistance

Satyagraha is the method of strong determination to stick to what is truth and right while passive resistance suggested something negative, conceived as the weapon of the weak, *Satyagraha* suggested the active principle of love.

> "*Satyagraha* differs" says Gandhi "from passive resistance as the North Pole from the South. The latter has been conceived as the weapon of the weak and does not exclude the use of physical force or violence for the purpose of gaining one's end. Whereas the former has been conceived as a weapon of the strongest and excludes the use of violence in any shape of form."[3]

Gandhi felt ashamed of using the word passive resistance wrongly attributing the qualities of *satyagraha*. Passive resistance is commonly understood in the west in its historical setting as weapon of the weak meant for the unarmed and helpless. A passive resister eschews violence not as a matter of principle but due to the lack of means of violence. Passive resistance is based on sheer expediency. A passive resister uses arms when available and if there is a reasonable chance of success. There is no scope for love in passive resistance. It cannot be used against those dear to us as it leads to distrust and disregard. Passive resister harasses the opponent and forces him to do the desired course of action. It is not proved to be serviceable and constructive.

Satyagraha to be genuine may be offered against one's wife or one's children, against rulers, against fellow citizens or even against the whole world. Such universal force does not make any destruction between kinsmen and strangers, young and old, man and woman, friend and foe. The force to be applied can never be physical and there is no room for violence in it. The only universal application would be *ahimsa* or love. *Satyagraha* is based on love – Love does not burn others but it burns itself. Therefore a *satyagrahi* will enjoy suffering even into death.[4]

Satyagraha is independent of material existence, even in its elementary form of physical force or violence. Violence is the negation of this great spiritual force. It can be welded by those who will entirely give up violence in any form. It is a force that may be used in political and domestic affairs. Its universal applicability is a demonstration of its permanence and invincibility. It can be used a like by all men, women and children. It is totally untrue to say that it is a force to be used only by the weak so long as they are not capable of meeting violence by violence. Only those who realize that there something in man superior to the brute nature in him and those the latter yields to it, can be come an effective *Satyagraha*. This force fights against violence, and therefore to tyranny, all injustice, what light is to darkness. In politics its use is based upon the immutable maxim that government of the people is possible so long as they consent either consciously or unconsciously to be governed.

Duragraha

Duragraha takes it for granted that what the person insists upon truth and justice. In *duragraha* the tactics adopted are similar to that of *satyagraha* but the essentials of *duragraha* are entirely different. It is opposed to the spirit of non-violence for coercive measures are adopted. The distinction between *satyagraha* and *duragraha* is similar to that of the notion of good and evil.

Qualifications of Satyagraha

Satyagraha prescribes certain qualifications to be possessed by a *satyagrahi*. *Satyagraha* presupposes self-discipline, self-control, self-purification and a reorganization social status in the person offering it. The object of *satyagrahi* is to convert but not to coerce the wrong doer. A *satyagrahi* must not harbour ill will against the evil doer. He will lover come evil by good, anger by love, untruth by truth and *himsa* by *ahimsa*. An evil may be converted by the article of faith.

Gandhi held that the following qualifications are essential for every *satyagrahi* in India:

1. He must have a living faith in God, for he is his only Rock.
2. He must believe in truth and non-violence as his creed and therefore have faith in the goodness of human nature which he expects to evoke by his truth and love expressed through his suffering.
3. He must be leading a chaste life and be ready and willing for the sake of his cause to give up his life and his possessions.
4. He must be a habitual *khadi*-weaver and spinner. This is essential for India.
5. He must be a teetotaller and be free from the use of other intoxicants in order that his reason may be always unclouded and his mind constant.
6. He must carry out with a willing heart all the rules of discipline as may he laid down from time to time.
7. He should carryout the jail rules unless they are specially devised to hurt his self-respect.[5]

Although a *satayagrahi* can operate silently, it requires a certain amount of action on the part of *satyagrahi.* He must first mobilize the public opinion against the evil and eradicate it by means of wide and intensive agitation. When public opinion is sufficiently aroused against a social abuse, even the tallest would not dare to practice or openly lend support to it. An awakened and intelligent public opinion[6] is the most potent weapon of *satyagrahi.*

A *satyagrahi* has to observe perfect charity, adopt poverty, follow truth and cultivate fearlessness. He regards the spinning wheel, village crafts etc. as the pillars of *ahimsa.* Besides observing non-violence with his parents, brothers, sisters, children and relatives and servants, he must be in a position to stand in the test at the time of political or communal disturbances or under the menace of thieves and decoits. Mere sacrifice is no good. It must be followed by some qualification.

In the event of any communal fights, he will not take sides. But he would assist only that party which is demonstrately in the right. As a Hindu he must be generous towards Muslims and will sacrifice himself if the situation demands in his attempt to save non-Hindu from a Hindu attack. [7] As a Hindu he must fraternize the Muslims and the rest. He must not make any distinction on the grounds of faith or religion without any fear. If a *satyagrahi* is qualified himself by his selfless service, he will make a fit offering of himself as a firm believer on non-violence in the event any communal conflagration. Similarly to meet he menace of thieves and dacoits, he will need to go among and cultivate friendly relations with the communities from which the thieves and dacoits generally come.

Conditions of *Satyagraha*

Mahatma Gandhi advocated the following conditions for the success of *satyagraha*:

1. The *satyagrahi* should not have any hatred in his heart against the opponent.
2. The issue must be true and substantial.
3. The *satyagrahi* must be prepared to suffer till the end of his cause". [8]

The *satyagrahi* must stand for the just cause without the use of violence. If violence is exercised the just cause is defeated. He should exclude the use of violence in any shape or form whether in thought, speech or deed. If the cause is just, with the capacity for endless and avoidance of violence. Victory is a certainty. Therefore, a *satyagrahi* cannot be resorted for personal gain but only for the good of others. *Satyagraha* cannot be resorted for personal gain but only for the good of others. *Satyagraha* can achieve any worthy object. It is the highest infallible means and the greatest force. *Satyagraha* rids society of all its political land economic.

The methods of *satyagraha* may be classified into four categories:

1. Purifactory,
2. Forms of non-cooperation,
3. Methods of civil disobedience and
4. The constructive programme.

All these methods may be employed by individual groups or mass movements in the political arena and in different spheres of social life. These methods are consistent with non-violence.

Civil Disobedience

Gandhi held that *satyagraha* in the political sphere assumes the form of civil disobedience. Gandhi defined civil disobedience as 'Civil breach of unmoral statutory enactments'. It seems that this word was coined by Henry Thoreau to signify his own resistance to the unjust laws of a slave state. Thoreau has left a masterly treatise on the duty of Civil Disobedience. Gandhi thought that Thoreau was perhaps not an out and out champion of non-violence. Thoreau probably limited his breach of his statutory laws to the revenue law, i.e. the payment of taxes but the term Civil Disobedience as practised in 1919 covered a breach of any statutory and unmoral law which signified the resisters out law in a civil, i.e., non-violent manner. Thoreau invoked the sanctions of law and cheerfully suffered imprisonment. Civil Disobedience presupposed the habit of obedience out of will to laws without fear of their sanctions.[9]

Gandhi said that Disobedience to be civil must be sincere respectful, restrained, never deferent, it must be based upon some well-understood principle. It must not be capricious. Above all it must not have ill-will or hatred behind it.[10]

> "The use of Civil Disobedience" says Gandhi, "will be healthy, necessary and effective only if we otherwise conform to the laws of all growth. We must therefore give its full and therefore greater value to the adjective 'civil' than to disobedience'. Disobedience without civility, discipline, discrimination, non-violence is certain destruction. Disobedience combined with love is the living water of life. Civil Disobedience is a beautiful variant to signify growth; it is not discordance which spells death".[11]

Gandhi held the opinion firmly that civil disobedience is the purest type of constitutional agitation. But it becomes degrading and despicable, it its civil, e.e., non-violent character is a more camouflage. If the honesty of non-violence be admitted, there is no warrant for condemnation even if it is of the fiercest disobedience.

> "Civil disobedience" says Gandhi, "is never followed by anarchy. Criminal disobedience can lead to it. Every State puts down criminal disobedience by force. It perishes of it does not. But put down civil disobedience is to attempt to imprison conscience. Civil disobedience can only lead to strength and purity. A civil resister never uses arms and hence he is harmless to a State that is at all willing to listen to the voice of public opinion. He is dangerous for an autocratic – State for he brings about is fall by engaging public opinion upon the matter for which he resists the State. Civil disobedience therefore becomes sacred duty when the State has become lawless or which is the same thing, corrupt. And a citizen that barters with such a State shares its corruption of lawlessness".[12]

Civil disobedience is conceived as the inherent rights of a citizen.[13] A *satyagrahi* obey the flaws of society out of his free will as he considers it to be his sacred duty to do so. When a person obeys the laws of society scrupulously, we would be in a position to judge which particular laws are good and jut and which laws are unjust and iniquitous. It is only then does the right accrue to him of civil disobedience of certain laws in certain well defined circumstances.[14]

Condition to be Observed

Gandhi held that the first indispensable condition precedent to any civil resistance is that there should be surety against the out break of violence either because of those identified with civil resistance or of general public. It is not answerable in the event of an out break of violence that has been instigating by the State or other agencies hostile to civil resistance. Civil resistance cannot flourish in an atmosphere of violence.[15]

Non-Cooperation

Non-Cooperation is a branch of *satyagraha*. It is not non-cooperation with the evil-doer but with his evil deed. The *satyagrahi* cooperates with the evil-doer in what is good, for he does not treat him as his enemy. By cooperating with him in what is not evil. *Satyagraha* wins him ever from evil.[16]

> "Non-cooperation" says Gandhi, "predominantly implies withdrawing of cooperation from the State that in the non-cooperators view has become corrupt and excludes Civil Disobedience of the fierce type".[17]

Non-cooperation includes all non-violent resistance for the vindication of truth. It may include strike, walkout, *hurtal* and resignation of offical titles and so on. Gandhi held that non-cooperation is an attempt to awaken the masses to a sense of their dignity and power.[18] It is a protest against an unwitting and unwilling participation in evil. In the words of Gandhi 'Non-cooperation with evil is as much as a duty as cooperation with good'.[19]

Non-cooperation is not a passive state but it is an intensively active state, more active than physical resistance or violence. It must be non-violent. Therefore, it is neither punitive nor based on malice, ill-will or hatred.[20]

Gandhi said that the duty of non-cooperation with unjust men and king's was strictly enjoined by all the religions who is same as the duty of cooperation with just men and kings. Most of the scriptures of the world seem even to go beyond non-cooperation and prefer violence to effeminate submission to a wrong.[21]

Fasting

Gandhi considered fasting as a potent weapon in the armory of *satyagraha*. He held that it cannot be taken by everyone. To observe fasting mare physical capacity is no qualification for it. It is of no use one needs to have a living faith on God. It should not be a mechanical effort or a mere imitation. It is because it should come from the depth of one's soul.[22] in a pure fast there is no room for selfishness, anger, lack of faith or impatience. Gandhi held that infinite patience, firm resolve, single-mindedness of purpose, perfect calm and without anger is absolutely necessary there. Since it is not possible for a person to develop all these qualities at one time, no one who has not devoted himself to following the laws of *ahimsa* should undertake a *satyagrahi* fast.[23]

Gandhi says that fasting is of fierce type which is altogether not free from danger. Gandhi condemned fast when it was found to be wrong or morally unjustified. But to shirk a fast when it has moral basis is a dereliction of duty. He held that such fast has to be based upon unadulterated truth and ahimsa.[24]

Fasting unto death is the last and the most potent weapon which is a sacred thing. It must be accepted with all its implications. It is not fast that matters but what it implies that matters.[25] Fasting cannot be undertaken mechanically. It is a powerful but dangerous if handled amateurishly. Complete self-purification is required.[26]

He held that fasts can be really coercive, but such fasts are to attain a selfish object.[27] A *satyagrahi* should fast only as a last resort when all other avenues of redress are explored and failed. He who has no inner strength should not dream of it. If a *satyagrahi* once undertakes a fast with firm conviction, he must stick to his resolve whether there is chance of his action bearing fruit or not. But this does not mean that fasting cannot or can bear fruit. He who fasts with the expectation of fruit generally fail. Every if he does not fail, the looses all the inner joy that a true fast holds.[28]

Constructive Programme

Gandhi stressed the need for *satyagraha* to engage in silent active, constructive work of reform and social service. He pointed out that the votaries of *satyagraha* must store up the necessary non-violent energy. They cannot become non-violent unless they undergo a process of corporate cleaning. This they can do only by engaging themselves in carrying out a self throughout constructive programme which requires a combined effort to promote common good. He later pointed out that the constructive work should be for its own sake. Yet it will develop the quality required for non-violent responsible government. The capacity to take political power will increase in exact proportion to the ability to achieve success in the constructive effort. It is only through such a constructive programme, that a system of non-violent self-rule could emerge.

Gandhi pointed out:

> This depends on individual workers, cultivating non-violence in thought, word lends deed, my means of a concerted effort in the fulfilment of the four-fold constructive programme. Maximum of work and

> minimum of speech must be your motor. In the centre of the programme is the spinning wheel – no haphazard programme of spinning, but scientific understanding ever detail, including the mechanics and mathematics of it, study of cotton and its varieties and so on. There is the programme of literacy. You must concentrate exclusively on it and not talk of any other thing.[29]

Constructive programme includes communal harmony, removal of untouchability, adult education and village improvement, peasant uplift, the development of non-violent labour unions, economic and social equality, decentralized economic production and distribution through the promotion of cottage and small scale industries and the abolition of various social evils.

Gandhi pointed out that Civil Disobedience could be most effective in the redress of local wrongs and in arousing the local conscience whereas it could never be directed for a general cause like constructive programme. Civil Disobedience is itself an aid to the constructive effort and a full substitute for armed revolt. The best training for proper civil disobedience is through the constructive programme.

In a *satyagraha* campaign the mode of fight and the choice of tactics to offer civil resistance or organize non-violent strength through constructive work and purely selfless humanitarian service are determined in accordance with the exigencies. A *satyuagrahi* must carry out whatever plan is laid out with a cool determination without excitement and depression.

REFERENCES

1. *Young India*, 23-3-1921.
2. *Ibid*, 14-1-1920.
3. *Ibid*, 14-1-1920, p. 142.
4. *Ibid*, 27-2-1930.
5. *Harijan*, 25-3-1939.

6. *Young India,* 19-3-1925.
7. *Ibid,* 27-2-1970.
8. *Harijan,* 31-3-1946, p. 64.
9. *Young India,* 23.3.1921.
10. *Ibid.,* 24-3-1920.
11. *Ibid.,* 5-1-1922.
12. *Ibid.,* 5-1-1922.
13. *Ibid.,* 5-1-1922.
14. M.K. Gandhi, *The Story of My Experiments with Truth,* p. 347.
15. *Harijan,* 18-3-1939, p. 53.
16. M.K. Gandhi, *Satyagraha,* Preface-IV.
17. *Young India,* 23-3-1921.
18. *Young India,* 1-12-1920.
19. *Ibid.,* 1-6-1921
20. *Ibid.,* 25-8-1920, p. 322.
21. *Ibid.,* 4-8-1920.
22. *Harijan,* 18-3-1939, p. 56.
23. *Ibid.,* 11-10-1940, p. 322.
24. *Harijan,* 28-7-1946, p. 235.
25. *Ibid.,* 18-81946, p. 262.
26. *Ibid.,* 27-101946, p. 272.
27. *Ibid.,* 9.9.1933, p. 5.
28. *Ibid.,* 21-4-1946, p. 93.
29. *Ibid.,* 10-6-1939.

7

Industrialization

The growth of industrialism has appeared to Gandhi as in the case of Ruskin and Tolstoy as a menace to realize the basic ideals of human society. Ruskin raised his voice against the degrading conditions of nineteenth century labour and the enslavement of man to the machine. Similar was the idea held by Tolstoy who said that the hateful industrialism has reduced the people to the state of slavery.

Industrialization depends upon the procurement of vast quantities of raw material coupled with a vast quantities of raw material coupled with a vast market for the sale of the finished goods.[1] Industrialization flourishes in an atmosphere where there are resources and markets of foreign countries. Exploitation of the underdeveloped countries, colonial expansion, imperialism, commercial monopoly, war with other industrialized countries, diplomatic mechanism for keeping down the political and economic growth of the rivals and the exploited nations, the propagation of the myth of cultural, racial and religious superiorities of the exploiters follow in a ceaseless train demoralizing the whole world.[2]

The growth of large scale industries is based on the investment of large capital and the employment of number of labourers. It breeds equally the large problems of the relation between capital land labour. Gandhi with disgust and horror could see the openly violent rebellions of labourers in other countries against the subtle violence of the capitalistic countries. He finds the same story being repeated in India in a few industrial areas. He held that it would not be wise for our country to try to establish and increase industrialism and invite all troubles that have already beset the industrialized countries.[3]

Gandhi found that the growth of big cities in some Indian cities attracted the villagers to the crowded cities. Many have drifted to the cities to improve their living conditions. This resulted the village homes to be broken. The healthy social ties and neighborly feelings had mostly gone. Individuals are lost in huge and rushing systems, the beginnings, ends and purposes of which are very dimply realized by him. Man is reduced to a mere tool. He lost his personality and his spontaneous moral sense. He scarcely feels the joy of creation enjoyed by the producer of a village handicraft. Life became a mechanical drudgery. Escape sought in grows sensual pleasures like drinking gambling and to all the vices that follow from them. The whole process of industrialized growth appeared to Gandhi as a monstrous process of mechanization, dehumanization and demoralization whereby individual could never realize the best in them.[4]

Before advent of the Industrial Revolution, workers used to buy their own raw materials, spun woven and sell the finished goods. But they could not compete with the new machinery. From the position of sculled craftsmanship, the workers have sunk to the position of 'hands in a factory'. Industrialism is a direct blow to the craftsman and dignity of labour. As a result, the worker is reduced to slavery.[5]

Civilization in the Modern Times

Gandhi held that the land in which we are living is made hideous by the smoke and the din of mill chimneys and factories and whose roadways are traversed by rushing engines, dragging numerous cars crowded with men. They do not know for most part what they are after, who are often absent minded. Their tempers do not improve. They are like sardines in boxes. Gandhi referred to all these as they are held to be symbolical of material progress. But they do not add an atom to the happiness of humanity.[6]

The present world is confronted with the evils of industrialism due to the crises of environmental pollution and the complete alienation or man from his work. It is feared that the structure of modern industrialism may slowly atrophy mankind.[7]

In the past when people wanted to fight with one another, they measured between them their bodily strength. But now it is possible to take away thousands of lives by one man working behind a gun from a hill. In the past, men worked in open air as much as they liked. But now thousands of workmen meet together and for the sake the maintenance they work in factories or mines. But their condition is reduced to that of beasts as they are obliged to work, at the risk of their lives, at most dangerous occupations for the sake of millionaires.

Gandhi could realize by experience that these instruments do not contribute to the man's spiritual progress. Their is no limit for man's ambition. He detested the need desire of men to destroy distance and time to increase animal appetites and to go to the ends of the earth in search of their satisfaction. He called this as satanic civilization.[9]

Gandhi considered this industrial civilization as a disease because it is all evil. Gandhi was not against telegraphs and steamships provided they run without the the support of industrialism, but people must not suffer exploitation for the sake of steamships and telegraphs. Gandhi held that they are in no way indispensable for the permanent welfare of the human race. He said that our concern should be to destroy industrialism at any cost. People are made rush in multiplying their wants vanity thinking that they add to the real substance and real knowledge of the world. When they retrace their steps they say 'what have we done'? Gandhi referred to Wallace, a contemporary of Darwin who said that fifty years of brilliant inventions and discoveries have not added an inch to the moral height of mankind.[10]

Industrialization - A Curse

Gandhi was afraid that industrialization would be a curse to the mankind. But exploitation of one nation by another cannot go on for all time. Industrialism flourishes in our atmosphere of man's capacity to exploit the foreign market being open to him and on the absence of competitors.[11] The life in Russia which has reached the state of apotheosis of industrialization is not appealing. Gandhi referred to the saying of Jesus in the *Bible*.

> 'What shall it avail a man if he gain the whole world and lose his soul'?

In the modern terms Gandhi said that it is beneath human dignity and become a mere cog in the machine. He wanted:

> Every individual to become a full-blooded and fully developed member of the society.[12]

Gandhi held that India should not take industrialism after the manner of the west. Unless the capitalists of our country help to avert the tragedy by becoming the trustees for the welfare of the masses by devoting their talents not for themselves but for the service of the masses in the spirit of altruism, they will end either by destroying the masses or being destroyed by them.[13]

Reinstatement of Man

For Gandhi the supreme consideration is man. The machine should not tend to atrophy the limbs of man.[14] He aimed at the disappearance of the achievements of the machine age so that the handicrafts would remain; when all exploitation has ceased, service and honest labour would remain.[15] He was clear in stating that while the machine age aims at converting men into machines, he aimed at reinstating man turned machine into his original estate.[16] Machine should extend man's ability but should not dominate him. It should supplement his limited physical effort but not completely supplant it.[17]

Gandhi considered machinery like a snake-hole which contains a number of snakes. Large cities exist when there is machinery and this is followed by tram-cars and railways, and electric light.

Gandhi held that as the result of the increase of artificial locomotion, the health of the people has suffered. He could not recall a single good point that contributed to the good of the machinery.[18]

Human Labour and Machine

Gandhi found that unlike in some countries where there is dearth of labour, machines are necessary for saving human labour. Our country has enough labourers. The only question is how to employ them.[19]

Gandhi pointed out:

> What I object a to is the craze for machinery, not machinery as such. The craze is for what they call labour saving machinery. Men go on saving labour till thousands are without work and thrown on the open streets to die of starvation. I want to save time and labour, not for a fraction of mankind, but for all.[20]

The machines can perform the work of more people. If there are unemployed persons, the use of machines that replaces persons adds to much more unemployment. So in country like ours wherein unemployment is more, the choice of machines must be such that they do not add further to the existing unemployment. So the technology has to be chosen in accordance with the location and there is need to set up of an appropriate technology.[21]

Technology has to be non-exploitative and its purpose has to uplift every human being. It should not encourage centralism. Romesh K. Diwan says that technology must fulfil the following four conditions. They are:

1. The operators must have full control of the technology,
2. The technology must not replace the worker,
3. The technology must increase the productivity of the workers, and
4. It must be productive of goods and services that are needed by the worker.[22]

The machinery has to add to man's capacity for labour to work with his hands. The machinery devised has to be suitable to man's requirements. He pointed out 'I am not opposed to machinery as such. I am opposed to machinery which displaces labour and leaves it idle'.[23] He held that saving of labour of the individual should be the object but it should not be out of human greed and motive. So Gandhi welcomed any day a machine to straighten crooked spindles. There is need to replace greed by love.[24]

Gandhi did not have consideration for such type of machinery which is meant to enrich a few at the expense of the many.[25] He stood against all destructive machinery. But he welcomed such machinery which has simple tools and instruments as it lightens the burden of millions of cottages.[26]

Gandhi opposed those machines which would displace human labour and would concentrate power in the hands of a few. He held that any machine that does not deprive the masses of the opportunity to labour and adds to the efficiency of the individual which a man can handle without becoming its slave has to be protected.

He pointed out:

> In this there is no room for machines that would displace human labour and that would concentrate power in a few hands. Labour has its unique place in a cultured human family. Every machine that helps every individual has a place.[27]

The conflict associated with man and machine prompted Gandhi to accept machinery of certain type on a limited scale. He noticed the improper use of machines which degraded man.

Wealth in the Hands of All

Gandhi opposed vehemently the concentration of wealth in the hands of a few at the exploitation of many. He pointed out:

> I want the concentration of wealth, not in the hands of a few, but in the hands of all. Today the machinery merely helps a few to ride on the backs of millions. The impetus behind it is not the philanthropy to save labour, but greed. It is against constitution of things that I am fighting with all my might.[26]

Gandhi held that the organization of machinery for the purpose of concentrating wealth and power in the hands of the exploitation of many was altogether wrong.[27] Much on the organization of machinery of the present age helps to be in the hands of a few. He suggested the movement of spinning-wheel was an organized attempt to displace machinery from the state of exclusiveness and exploitation and to place it in its proper state. Under the scheme proposed by Gandhi, men in-charge of machinery would think not of themselves of even of the nature but of the whole human race.[30] He held that machinery to well used has to help and ease human effort. But the machinery in the present use tends more and more to concentrate wealth in the hands of a few in total disregard of millions of men and women who are deprived of their food.[31]

So efforts have to be made to relieve the miseries and the evils of the people associated with industrialization. The poor Man's Guardian of 1835 carried the following remark.

> While the worker produces all the wealth, he is obliged to content himself with the merge share necessary to support his existence and the surplus goes to the capitalist who with the King the priests, lords, esquires and gentlemen, lives upon the labour of the working man.[32]

Gandhi held that when production and consumption are localized, the temptation to speed up production, indefinitely and at any price disappears. All the difficulties and problems that the present day economic system presents too will come to an end. "There would be no unnatural accumulation of hoards in the pockets of the few and want in the midst of plenty in disregard of the rest" says Gandhi.[33]

Under the economic system advocated by Gandhi labour is the current coin but not metal. Any person who is capable of using his labour, has that coin and wealth. He converts his labour into cloth and grain. He said that it is exchange of labour on free, fair and equal terms. So there is no robbery. This should not be objected to and be thought of as a reversion to the primitive system of barter. International trade is based on the barter system.[34]

Type of Machinery

It should not be supposed that Gandhi was opposed to machines. He says:

> Machinery has its place; it has come to stay. But it must not be allowed to displace necessary human labour.[35]

He was conscious that even the spinning-wheel he tried to introduce in every Indian home was a machine. He always encouraged for its improvement. He said that an improved plough is a good thing. But if by chance one man could plough up by some mechanical invention of the whole land of our country and control the produce of agriculture and if the millions had no other occupation, they would starve. He welcomed every improvement in the cottage machine which does not displace the hand labour and ready to give millions of farmers some other occupation in their homes.[36] He would prize any invention of science made for the benefit of all.[37] He said that if mankind were to progress and realize the ideal of equality and brotherhood, it must adopt and act on the principle of *Unto This Last*.[38]

Alternatives

Gandhi held that the introduction of labour saving machines would result in more unemployment. It would deprive the work of those who are engaged in manual work, cottage industries and agriculture in the villages. The services of unemployed labourers could only be utilised by starting of other industries to manufacture other kinds of goods and so on. The effect would be to multiply the evils of industrialization. The newly developing industries would be mostly devoted to the production of luxury goods, creating more and more the insatiable demand for creative comforts. The motto then would become 'High living and plain thinking'.[39] Gandhi held that high thinking is inconsistent with material life.[40] The welfare of humanity lies in 'plain living and high thinking', but not in the multiplication of wants. It contains in curtailing the dispensable desires and in devoting maximum energy to the pursuit of spiritual values.[41]

State Control

Gandhi believed at the same time that some key industries as necessary. He pointed out:

> The heavy machinery for work of public utility which cannot be undertaken by human labour has its inevitable place, but all that would be owned by the State and used entirely for the benefit of the people.[42]

These key industries should have state ownership, wherein a large number of people have to work together. The ownership of the products of their labour whether skilled or unskilled would vest in them through the state. It is only when such a state is based on non-violence. He said that he would not dispossess moneyed, men by force, but would invite their cooperation in the process of conversion to state ownership.[43]

Rural Industries

Gandhi aimed at the revival of rural industries that are. Capable of being revived. The revival of the village industries is possible only when they are no more exploited. Industrialization on a mass scale would necessarily lead to passive or active exploitation of the villagers as the problem of competition and marketing come in. Gandhi aimed at concentrating on the village being self-contained which would mainly manufacture for use. If such character of the village industry is maintained, there would be no objection for the villagers to use even the modern machines and tools that they can make and can afford to use. But they should not be used as a means for the exploitation of others.[44]

Gandhi endorsed the proposition that any plan which exploits the raw materials of a country and neglects potentially more powerful manpower is lopsided. It cannot tend to establish human equality. He held that real planning consists in the best utilizations of the whole manpower of

India and the distribution of the raw products of India in her numerous villages instead of sending them outside and to rebury finished articles at fabulous prices.[45]

REFERENCES

1. *Young India,* 12-11-1031, p. 355.
2. D.M. Datta, *The Philosophy of Mahatma Gandhi,* p. 112.
3. *Ibid.,* pp. 112-13
4. *Ibid.,* p. 113.
5. Holling Worth, G.E. (ED), Sesame and Lillies, *Preface,* p. XII.
6. *Speeches and Writings of Mahatma Gandhi,* pp. 354-55.
7. J.D. Sethe, *Gandhi Today,* p. 4.
8. M.K. Gandhi, *Hind Swaraj,* pp. 36-37.
9. *Young India,* 17-3-1927, p. 85.
10. *Ibid,* 8-12-1927, p. 414.
11. *Ibid,* 12-11-1931, p. 355.
12. *Harijan,* 28-1-1939, p. 438.
13. *Young India,* 20.12.1928. p. 422.
14. *Ibid.,* 13.11.1924. p. 378.
15. *Harijan,* 30.11.193 5. p. 3 29.
16. *Ibid.,* 29.8.1936. p. 228.
17. Ram K. Vepa, *New Technology: A Gandhian Concept,* p.102.
18. M.K. Gandhi, *Hind Swaraj,* p. 96.
19. *Harijan,* 16.11.19 34. p. 316.
20. *Young India,* 13.11.1924. p. 378.
21. *Gandhi Marg,* Vol. IV. Oct. 1982, p. 644.
22. *Ibid.,* p. 643.
23. *Harijan,* 15.9.19 46. p. 310.
24. *Young India,* 13.11.1924. p. 378.
25. *Harijan,* 22.6.1935. p. 146.
26. *Young India,* 17.6.1926 p..218
27. *Harijan.* 28.7.1946. p. 236
28. *Young India,* 13.11.1924. p. 376,
29. *Ibid.,* 17.9.1925. p. 321.

30. *Ibid.*,
31. *Harijan,* 14.9.1935. p. 244.
32. Milliken, E.K., *The Victorian Era.* p. 91.
33. *Harijan,* 2.11.1934. p. 302.
34. *Ibid.*
35. *Young India,* 5.1.1925. p. 377.
36. *Ibid.*, 5.1.1925. p. 377.
37. *Harijan,* 22.6.1935. p. 146
38. *Ibid.*, 25.8.1946. p. 281.
39. D.M. Datta, *The Philosophy of Mahatma Gandhi.* p.144.
40. *Harijan,* 1.9.1946. p. 285.
41. D.M. Datta, *op.cit.*, p. 144.
42. *Harijan,* 22.6.1935. p. 146.
43. *Ibid.*, 1.9.1946. p. 285.
44. *Ibid.*, 28.9.1946. p. 226.
45. *Ibid.*, 23.3.1947. p. 79.

8

Social System and Current Problems

Gandhi considered the reform of society as the integral part of the process of reform of the individual. For him individual is the starting point of social regeneration. Gandhi was opposed to the irrational cultural traditions and meaningless customs traditions and relations of the Hindu society.

Untouchability

Untouchability is an inhuman institution in Hindu society as the mere touch of an untouchable was sin. Sensitive to this inhuman practice, Gandhi rebelled against this outrage of human personality and campaigned against the evil of untouchability. He identified himself with the untouchables and called them with the name 'Harijan' which means man of God.

Gandhi believed in the spiritual oneness of all life as a Vedantist and a *Vaishnava*. So he was absolutely opposed to untouchability. The eradication of untouchability from the grass root level was a matter of atonement for the sins of the cruel sections of the Hindu world. He earnestly pleaded for the real brotherly embrace. He felt that the virus of untouchability was a curse causing deep agony to him. Gandhi appeared as a revolutionary leader. He preached social equality to the conservative Hindu India. His campaign against the untouchability was in recognition of the human rights. He confessed honestly that his fight against the deadly sin of untouchability was a fight against the impure inhumanity.[1]

Love of the people made him to stand against untouchability since his early life. From the day his mother said that he should not touch an untouchable, revolt began in his life.[2] In battling against untouchability and in dedicating himself to that battle Gandhi was ambitious to see a complete regeneration of humanity.[3]

Gandhi was wedded to the work for the extinction of untouchability long before he was wedded to his life. When there was a choice between working for the untouchable and remaining with his wife, he preferred the first. In his Ashram, which he considered as his family, he had several untouchables and a sweet but naughty girl living as his own daughter.[4]

The concern and passion for the untouchables was so much for Gandhi that he wanted to be reborn as an untouchable to share their sorrows and sufferings.

> "I do not want to be reborn" says Gandhi. "But if I have to be reborn, I should be born an untouchable, so that I may share their sorrows, sufferings and the affronts levelled against them in order that I may endeavour to free myself and them from that miserable condition. I therefore, prayed that if should be born again, I should do so not as a Brahmin, Kshatriya, Vaisya or Shudra, but as an *Atishudra*.[5]

Gandhi felt that the caste Hindu owed a sacred duty to the so-called untouchable. He must humble himself and become a *bhangi* (sweeper) to realize this in action. He stood for one united family to grow.

> "The ulcer of untouchability" says Gandhi, "has gone so deep down that it seems to pervade our life. Hence the unreal differences Brahman and Non-Brahmana, Provinces and provinces religion. Why should there be all this poison smelling of untouchability, why should we not all be children of one Indian family and further of one human family? Are we not the branches of the same tree? When untouchability is rooted out, these destructions will vanish and no one will consider himself superior to any other. Naturally exploitation too will cease and cooperation will be the order of the day."[6]

Gandhi aimed at reforms in Hinduism for the removal of untouchability. He considered the removal of untouchability as the greatest thing and a spiritual process.[7]

He told that is not enough to merely hold the belief passively that untouchability is a crime. He was of that he who is a passive spectator of crime is really and in law, an active participator in it. So there is need to begin and continue the agitation along all lawful and legitimate lines.[8]

Inter-dining and Inter-caste Marriage for the Removal of Untouchability

Gandhi said at one time, that interdining was not an essential part of the campaign for the removal of untouchability. But there was change in his attitude and said that he was for it and would encourage it. He went even further.[9] He went to the extent of saying that if

Untouchability lives, Hinduism must die.[10]

> "Untouchability" says Gandhi, "in the form we know is a canker eating into the very vitals of Hinduism. Dining and marriage restrictions stunt Hindu society. I think the destruction is fundamental. It would be unwise in a hurricane campaign to over weight and thus endanger the main issue. It may even amount to a breach of faith with the masses to call upon suddenly to view the removal of untouchability in a light different from what

> they have been height to believe it to be. On the one hand therefore, whilst inter-dining may go on where the public is itself ready for it, it, should not be part of an India-wide campaign."[11]

Gandhi had been pursuing a vigorous but cautions approach in his campaign against untouchability.

In reply to a question whether the Congress programme for the abolition of untouchability is included with inter-dining and inter-marriage he said:

> So far as I know the Congress nuied today, there is no opposition to dining with Harijans. But speaking for myself, I have said that we have all to become Harijans today or we will not be able to purge our selves completely of the taint of untouchability. I, therefore tell all boys and girls who want to marry that they can not be married at Sevagram Ashram unless one of the parties is a Harijan. I am convinced that there is no real difficulty in this. All that is needed is a change of outlook.[12]

V.P. Varma pointed out

> His successful struggle against the dark sin of untouchability will always be regarded as a vital contribution to Indian civilization and culture. He had the boldness to fight against a system and a prejudice sanctioned by centuries of old conservation.[13]

His crusade against untouchability, and his leadership of the Indian independence movement were based on ideals of social and political justice.[14]

Varnashrama Dharma

Varnashrama Dharma defines about the man's mission on this earth. He is not born to amass riches and explore the different means of livelihood. But man is born to utilize every atom of his energy for the purpose of knowing his Maker. It restricts him to the occupation of his forefathers.[15]

Gandhi believes in *varna* which is based on hereditary occupations. There are four *varnas* to mark four universal occupations - imparting knowledge, defending the defenseless, carrying on agriculture and commerce and performing service through physical labour. These occupations are common to all mankind. But Hinduism has recognized them as the low of human of existence. So it has made use of it in regulating social relations and conduct.

Gandhi holds that the abuse of varna resulted in innumerable casts with unnecessary and harmful restrictions for inter-marriage and inter-dining. But the *varna* has got nothing to do with these restrictions. He is of the opinion that the people of different *varnas* may inter-marry and inter-line. These restrictions may be followed by chastily and hygiene. A Brahmin who marries a Shudra girl or vice-versa commits no offence against the law of *varnas*.[16]

Gandhi believes that every man in this world is born with certain natural tendencies and limitations which he cannot overcome. The law of *varna* is deduced from a careful observation of those limitations. It establishes certain spheres of action for certain people which avoids all unworthy competition. While recognizing limitations, the law of *varna* does not admit of any distinction of high and low. On the other hand, it guarantees to each, the fruit of his labours. This great law is degraded and fallen into dispute. His conviction is that an ideal of social order will only be evolved when the implications of this law are fully understood and given effect to.[17]

Gandhi says that Brahmins and Kshatriyas, Vaishyas and Shudras are mere lables. He finds that there is utter confusion of *varna*. He wishes that all the Hindus be voluntarily called themselves Shudras. He is of the opinion that it is the only way to demonstrate the truth of Brahminism and to revive *varnashrama* in its true sense.[18]

Gandhi holds that *varna* is intimately if not indissolubly connected with birth and the observance of the law of *varna* means following the hereditary and traditional calling of our forefathers in spirit of duty.[19]

> "Varna" says Gandhi, "is determined by birth, but can be retained only observing its obligations. One born of Brahmana parents will be called a Brahmana, but if his life fails to reveal the attributes of a Brahmana when he comes of age, he cannot be called a Brahmana. He will have fallen from Brahmanahood. On the other hand one who is born not a Brahmana, but reveals in his conduct the attributes of a Brahmana will be regarded as a Brahmana, through he himself is claim the label.'[20]

If *varna* reveals the law of one's being and the duty that one has to perform, it confers no right. Thereby the idea of superiority or inferiority is wholly repugnant to it. He holds that all *varnas* are equal since the community depends no loss on one than on another. But today, *varna* means gradations of high and low. He fines it to be a hideous travesty of the original.[21]

Gandhi interprets Varnashramadharma in the following words.

"Varnashrama as I interpret it, satisfies the religious social and economic needs of a community. It satisfies the religious needs, because a whole community accepting the law is free to devote ample time of spiritual perfection. Observance of the law obviates social evils and entirely prevents the killing economic competition ... when people in disregard of the law mistake duties for privileges and try to pick and choose. Occupation for self-advancement, it leads to confusion of *Varna* and ultimate disruption of society. In this law there is no question of compelling any person to follow the parental occupation against his or her aptitude that is to say, there can be no compulsion from without as there was none for,

perhaps, several thousand years, during which, the law of *Varnashrama* worked without interruption. By training, the people had recognized the duty and the justice of the law, as they voluntarily lived under it".[2]

The society is treated as an organism and it is much familiar in traditional Indian thought. The *varna* scheme of social organization is for an organism interpreta-tion as society is conceived as a unit consisting of differentiated classes, each functioning in its specific sphere for the good of the entire society.[23]

Caste and Varna

Gandhi considered the four divisions to be fundamental, natural and essential. He felt that the innumerable sub-castes are sometimes a convenience and often a hindrance. It would be better if there is a fusion.

Gandhi was of the opinion that *varna* has got nothing to do with caste. The monster of caste masquerades in the guise of varna. It is this travesty of *varna* that has degraded Hinduism and India. The failure of following the law of *varna* resulted in both the economic and spiritual ruin.[24]

Mahatma Gandhi was profoundly influenced by Hindu philosophy. He had implicit faith in the basic kernels of Hinduism. Though he was a reformer, he did not reject any essentials of Hinduism. He stood for asterism but not for its perversion. In 1921 he wrote:

> From the economic point of view, its value was once very great. It ensured hereditary skill, it limited competition. It was the best remedy against pauperism. And it had all the advantages of trade guilds. Although it did not foster adventure or invention there, it is not known- to have come in the way either.
>
> Historically speaking, caste may be regarded as man's experiment or social adjustment in the Laboratory of

> Indian Society. If we can prove it to be a success, it can be offered to the world avarice and greed.[25]

The vast organization of caste answered the religious as well as the political needs of the community. The villagers managed their internal affairs through the caste system. Through caste system they could deal with any oppression from the ruling power. He holds that it is not possible to deny of a nation that was capable of producing the caste system and its power of organization.[26]

Gandhi did not believe in caste in the modern sense. It is a handicap to progress. He held that all are absolutely equal but the equality is of souls but not of bodies. Hence it is a mental state. There is need to realize equality in the midst of this apparent external inequality. He considered the assumption of superiority by any person over any other person as sin. If caste connotes any distinction in status, it is an evil.[27]

Gandhi held that *varnashrama dharma* in the *Shastras* as non-existent in the true sense of the term. The present caste system is quite contrary to *Varnashrama*. It would be better if public opinion abolishes it sooner.[28]

Gandhi made a distinction between religion and caste and asserted that caste has got nothing to do with religion and it is harmful to both spiritual and national growth.[29] He found that caste distinctions had taken deep root infecting the Muslims, Christians and followers of other religions in India. In fact class barriers are also to be found more or less in other parts of the world. This is a common feature found in the human race which can be eliminated only by the inculcation of religion in its true sense. Gandhi did not find any sanction for such barriers and destructions in the scriptures of any religion.[30]

The Status of Women

Gandhi holds that man and woman are equal in life. So

their problems must also be one in essence. Both lead the same life with same feelings and complement to each other. Both are interdependent, cannot live without the other's active life.[31]

> "Women" says Gandhi, "is the compassion of man, gifted with equal mental capacities. She has the right to participate in every minutest detail in the activities of man and she has an equal right of freedom and liberty with him. She is entitled to a supreme place in her own sphere of activity as man is in his. This ought to be the natural condition of things and not as a result only of learning to read and write."[32]

Since the times immemorial, man has dominated woman in some form or the other. Thereby woman has developed some kind of inferiority complex and formed the impression that she is inferior to man. But the seers among men have recognized her equal status with man.

Gandhi brings at the vital differences between man and woman. Although both are fundamentally one, it is true that there is a vital difference between the two. So the vocations of the two must be different. The duty of motherhood is undertaken by the vast majority of women. Women is passive whereas man is active. Man is the bread winner and the woman is the mistress of the house. She is the keeper of the house and serves bread. She is the care-taker. It is the sole prerogative of the woman to bring up the infants of the race without whose care, the race becomes extinct. Woman is the incarnation of non-violence (*ahimsa*) and love.[33]

Gandhi refers to the household functions of both man and woman which are at variance. Although man and woman are equal in life, but their functions differ. Women's right is to rule the home and man is the master outside it. Man earns and woman saves a part of it and spends the remaining for the family. She feeds and shapes the future of the child. The child learns at first from his mother. She is an educator to her children and hence mother to the Nation. After a certain period, a father ceases to influence his son but the mother never abdicates her place. The son after attaining manhood will play with the mother as he used to do when he was a child but he cannot do the same with his father.[34]

Gandhi is of the opinion that woman should not labour under legal disability not suffered by man. He says that both the sons and daughters have to be treated on the same footing of perfect equality. When woman begins to realize her strength in proportion to the education she receives, she will naturally resent the glaring inequalities for which she is subjected to. The removal of legal inequality is a mere palliative but the root evil lies much deeper than most people realize.[35] It has in man's abnormal desire for power and fame and still could be found in the mutual lust. It is the privilege of the awakened women to spot out and eradicate the age long evils.[36] When woman is freed from the man's snares, she rises to the full height and rebels against man's legislation and institutions designed by him. Her rebellion no doubt non-violent will be nevertheless effective.[37]

> "To call women", says Gandhi, "the weaker sex is a libel; it is man's injustice to woman. If by strength is meant, brute strength, then indeed is woman less brute than man. If by strength is meant moral powers then woman is immeasurably man's superior has she not greater intuition; is she not more self-sacrificing, has she not greater powers of endurance, has she not greater courage? Without her man could not be. Life non-violence is the law of our being, the future is with woman... who can make a more effective appeal to the heart than woman?

Gandhi holds that woman is the personification/self-sacrifice but unfortunately the woman does not realize the tremendous advantage she has over man. If she realizes the strength of non-violence/ she could not consent to be called the weaker sex.[38]

Gandhi believes in giving proper education for women. He is of the opinion that woman will not make her contribution to the world by just imitating or running a race with man. She can compete with man but will not rise to the great heights she is capable of by imitating man. He says that 'she can be the complement of man.'[39]

Gandhi states that woman must cease to consider herself the object of man's lust and must refuse to adorn herself for men including her husband if she wishes to be an equal partner.[40] Women have to refuse to be the slaves of their whims and fancies and the slaves of men. He advises women to refuse to decorate themselves and not to go in for scents and lavender waters. If women want to give out fragrance, it must come out of their heart.[41]

Thereby they can captivate not men but humanity. Gandhi holds that it is the women's birthright for man is born woman. He is flesh of her flesh and bone of her bone.[42] The woman who knows and fulfils her duty, realizes her dignified status. She is the queen but not the slave of the household.[43]

Gandhi makes no distinction between man and woman. He holds that woman should feel just as independent as man. Bravery is not alone man's monopoly.[44] He emphasizes the need to have independent thinking for women. Without independent thinking, they cannot think of their rights. The women have to be imparted practical education. Such type of teaching makes women to think independently and release them from the chains of caste that bind them so as to bring about a change in them. The world compel men to realize women's strength and capacity for sacrifice and give her places of honour.[45]

Gandhi finds no occasion for women to consider they subordinate or inferior to men. Languages proclaim that woman is half of man and it rationally follows that man is half of woman. They are not separate. The English language goes further and calls woman the better half of man. He advises women to resort to evil rebellion against all undesirable and unworthy restraints. The restraints that are beneficial must be voluntary.[46]

Gandhi pointed out

> Man should learn to give place to women and a community or country in which women are not honoured cannot be considered as civilized.[47]

Prohibition

Gandhi aims at a total prohibition to save the people from the curse. He holds that liquor is not a matter to trifle with. Soft and easy going policy will not cope with the tremendous evil.[48]

Drinks and drugs degrade those who are addict to them. The drunkard forgets the distinction between wife, mother and sister. He indulges in heinous crimes which about he feels ashamed during his sober moments.[49] Gandhi says that drink and drugs undermine the moral well-being and the lives of those who are given to this habit are in secure. Such of these women whose husbands are drunkards know the havoc the evil of drink works in homes that were one time orderly and peace giving.[50]

The evil caused by the drinks and the drug says Gandhi, is in many respects infinitely worse than the evil by malaria and the like. While the malaria injures the body only, the drink saps both body and soul.[51] Gandhi holds that drinking spirituous liquors in India to be more criminal than the petty thefts which the starving men and women commit for which they are prosecuted and punished. He advocates the summary punishment of those who manufacture the fiercy liquid and these even who will persist in drinking despite the repeated warnings. He does not hesitate to forcible prevent his children from rushing into fire or deep waters. Man's rush to red water is far more dangerous than rushing to a furnace or flooded stream.[52]

Gandhi finds drunk to be of a more disease than a vice. Most of the people would gladly leave the drink if they could.[53]

Gandhi prefers India to be reduced to a state of pauperism rather than to have thousands of drunkards to be in our midst.[54] He points out:

> Nothing but ruin stares a nation in the face that is a prey to the drink habit. History records that empires have been destroyed through that habit.[55]

Gandhi has become a staunch opponent of alcohol because of the painful experience he had in South Africa. The alcoholics were seen in a most pathetic condition. They waste all their earnings in drinking and their lives become devoid of any grace. The lives of several princes have been ruined by liquor. The condition of labour is pitiable. He observes:

> In a nutshell, alcohol ruins one physically, morally, intellectually and economically.[56]

Gandhi refers to the factory workers who do not drink before they come to work in factories. The conditions and environment they are placed in are such that they become addict to the habit of drink but they do not justify it.[57] The conditions to which the workers are reduced to such deplorable conditions because of the drink. The workers are forlorn and uncared for. The environment where they lead their life control the majority of the people.[58] His identification with labour made him to understand the great ruin the drink has brought to the homes of labourers. They would not touch liquor if it is not within reach. His eldest son who was intelligent, brave, patriotic and sacrificing was ruined by the drink habit. He is lost to his parents and society.[59]

The question of drink deals with a growing social evil. The state has to act against this when there is an opportunity. Prohibition is indispensable undoubtedly and the beginning of the reform. The drinker does not stop a long as the shop is near his door step to tempt him.[60] The constructive effort is doomed to failure if it is not preceded by total prohibition. As long, as the state permits and provides facilities for the addict to satisfy his craving, the reformer has little chance of success. His experience in South Africa tells, that the majority of the poor addicts could not resist the tempta-tion to enter the palatial bars that faced them. State prohibition is only the indispensable beginning but not the end of this great temperance reform.[61]

Gandhi pleads that social workers cannot work effectively so long as licensed liquor dens continue to lure the drinkers to enter them.[62]

The infortunate men who have become slaves to the habit require to be helped against themselves. Gandhi does not support the idea that facilities should be provided, to such of those who drink. The state does not cater to the vices of its people and such ill fame things should not be regulated or given license. He asks the country men to join the country in sweeping out the existence of the drink revenue and abolition of the liquor shops.[63]

There is no prohibition because drink brings a large revenue to the government. Even the Indian Ministers say that they cannot forego the revenue.[64]

> "If I were appointed dictator" says Gandhi, "for one hour for all India, the first thing I would do would be to close without compensation all the liquor shops, destroy all the toddy shops ... compel factory owners to produce humane conditions for their workmen and open refreshment and recreation rooms where these workmen would get innocent drinks and equally innocent amusements. ...[65]

Gandhi is of the opinion that many are skeptical about prohibition to be achieved as the financial lure will be too strong for them to resist. Some argue that the addicts will procure their drinks and drugs any how. When it is discovered that prohibition is a mere loss of revenue without any appreciable diminution in the consumption, they will revert the tainted revenue though illicit. Then the state will be worse than the present.

Gandhi does not share the fear of the loss of revenue to the State. He believes that there is the requisite moral momentum in the nation to achieve the noble end. To make prohibition a reality, a beginning has to be made at the earliest. Such of the states which lagged behind are bound to follow suit to the inevitable. There is need to expect for the sympathy and support not only of all parties of India including the Europeans/ but the best mind of the whole world. This may be considered as the greatest moral movement of the century.[66]

Gandhi says that the revenue received from the drink and drugs is a form of extremely degrading taxation. Taxation to be healthy must return ten-fold to the tax payer in the form of services. Excise makes people to play for their own corruption. He holds that the loss of revenue is only apparent. If this degrading tax is removed, this would enable the drinker, i.e., the tax payer to earn and spend better. It is a substantial economic gain to the nation.[67]

Gandhi suggests unhesitatingly cutting out the educational budget which purpose mainly the excise revenue is used to make up the loss of revenue caused by prohibition. He maintains that education can be made self-supporting But it cannot be made within a day even if the possibility of making education self-supporting is accepted. Other sources of revenue have to be tapped. Death duties, tax on tobacco have been given as some suggestions. If these are considered impossible for the immediate accomplishment, short term loans may be devised to tide over the deficit failing which the Central Government should be approached to curtail the military budget and give the provinces the appropriate grant. The demand would be irresistible especially if it is demonstrated by the provincial govern-ments that they do not need the military for the existing internal peace and tranquility.[68]

Gandhi is of the opinion that the voluntary organizations especially manned by women work in the labour areas who would visit those who are addicted to drink and try to wean-ling them from the habit. The employers who employ by low labour are expected to provide cheap, healthy refreshment, reading and entertainment rooms, where the working men can go and find shelter, knowledge, health, giving food and drink and innocent fun. By this it could be understood, that prohibition means a type of adult education of the nation and not merely a closing down of grog shops.

Prohibition he holds, should begin by preventing any new shop from being licensed and closing some that are in danger of becoming a nuisance to the public. Gandhi describes the total prohibition in the following words:

> Total prohibition is prohibition against sales of intoxicating drinks and drugs, except under medical prescription by a practitioner licensed for the purpose and to be purchasable only at Government depots maintained therefor.[69]

Gandhi holds that prohibition implies new life for many millions. It is a new and substantial accession of moral and material strength. The fact that honest prohibition gives a dignity and prestige to the Congress which perhaps no other single step could give, needs to be realized. There is need to observe that prosecution of prohibition means identification with the masses and a resolute determination to refuse to have anything to do with the drink revenue. He maintains that by delaying the prohibition for the sake of revenue, the Congress government breaks up the spirit if not the latter of their pledge.[70]

> "If then" says Gandhi, "prohibition is to mean a great moral awakening in India/ the closing of liquor shops would merely mean the indispensable beginning of the movement ending in the complete weaning from drink and narcotics of those poor people and some rich people whom the habit has ruined body and soul."[71]

REFERENCES

1. V.P. Varma, *The Political Philosophy of Mahatma Gandhi*, p. 111
2. *Harijan*, 24.12.1938. p. 393.
3. *Ibid.*, 25.3.1933. p. 3.
4. *Young India*, 5.11.1931. p. 341.
5. *Ibid.*, 4.5.1921. p. 144.
6. *Harijan*, 10-2-1946, p. 4.
7. *Young India*, 6.1.19 27. p. 2.
8. *Ibid.*, 20.10.1927. p. 353.
9. *Harijan*, 28.7.1946. p. 234.
10. *Ibid.*, 28.9.1947. p. 349.
11. Pyarelal, *The Epic Fast*, pp. 314-15.
12. Nirmal Kumar Bose, *Selections From Gandhi*, p. 268.
13. V.P. Varma, *The Political Philosophy of Mahatma and Sarvodaya*, pp.111-12.
14. *Ibid.*, p. 236.
15. *Young India*, 27.10.1927. p. 357.
16. *Ibid.*, 4.6.1931. p. 129.
17. *Modern Review*, Oct. 1935. p. 413
18. *Harijan*, 25.3.1933. p. 3.
19. *Young India*, 20.10.1927. p. 357
20. *Harijan*, 28.9.1934. p. 260.
21. *Ibid.*, 28.9.1934. p. 261.
22. *Ibid.*, 4*3.1933. p. 5.

23. Buddhadeva Bhattacharyya, *Evolution of the Political Philosophy of Gandhi*, p. 174.
24. *Young India*, 24.11.1927. p. 390.
25. *Ibid.*, 5.1.1921. p. 2.
26. *Speeches and Writings of Mahatma Gandhi*, p. 339.
27. *Young India*, 4.6.1931. p. 129.
28. *Harijan*, 16.11.1935. p. 316.
29. Nirmal Kumar Bose, *Selections From Gandhi*, p. 265.
30. *The Hindu Daily Newspaper*, 19.9.1945.
31. *Harijan*, 24.2.1940. p. 13.
32. *Speeches and Writings of Mahatma Gandhi*, p. 425.
33. *Harijan*, 24.2.1940. p. 13.
34. *Collected Works of Mahatma Gandhi*, Vol.XIV. p. 31
35. *Young India*, 17.10.1929. p. 340.
36. *Ibid.*, 17.10.1929. p. 340
37. *Ibid.*, 16.4.1925. p. 133.
38. *Ibid.*, 10.4.1930. p.121.
39. *Ibid.*, 14.1.1932. p. 19.
40. *Harijan*, 27.2.1937. p. 19.
41. *Young India*, 21.7.1921. p.229.
42. *Ibid*, 8.12.1927. p.406
43. *Harijan*, 12.10.1934. p.277.
44. *Ibid.*, 5.1.1947. p.478.
45. *Ibid.*, 21.4.1946. p. 96.
46. *Ibid.*, 23.3.1947. p. 80.
47. *Ibid.*, 11.1.1948. p. 508.
48. *Young India*, 16.4.1925. p.136.
49. *Ibid.*, 4.2.1926. p. 49.
50. *Ibid.*, 10.4.1930. p.121.
51. *Ibid.*, 3.3.1927. - p. 68.
52. *Idid.*, 8.8.1929. p.264.
53. *Ibid.*, 6.7ol921. p.210.
54. *Ibid.*, 15.9.1927. p.306.
55. *Ibid.* 11.4.1929. £.115.
56. M.K. Gandhi. *Key to Health*, pp.3 5-6.

57. *Young India.* 18.4.19 29. p.122.
58. *Ibid.*, 8.9.19 27. p.296.
59. *Harijan,* 3.6.1939. p.148.
60. *Ibid.*, 14.8.1937. p.212.,
61. *Ibid,* 25.9.1937. p.272.
62. *Ibid,* 17.6.1939. p.164.
63. *Young India,* 8.6.19 21. p.181.
54. *Ibid.*, 18.4.1929. p.122,
65. *Ibid.*, 25.6.1931. p.155.
66. *Harijan,* 28.8.1937. p.228.
67. *Ibid.*, 31-7-1937, 9. 196.
68. *Ibid.*, 28-8-1937, p. 229.
69. *Harijan,* 31.7.1937. p.196.
70. *Ibid.*, 24.12.1938. p.396.
71. *Ibid.*, 28.8.1937. p.228.

9

Gandhi's Views on Education

Education means, "To nourish", "To bring up" and "To raise." This means educating a child, nourishing or bringing out a child in accordance with norms, ends or aids. It also implies to lead out or to draw out. This means educating a child or drawing out what is ingrained in child or to lead out of darkness into light. Ancient Indian thinkers viewed education as idealistic or spiritualistic whereas the modern Indian thinkers regard education from the practical standpoint. In *Rigveda* education has been understood as something that makes man self-reliant and selfless. In the Upanishadic thought education has been regarded, as a means to attain salvation. Sankaracharya considers education as realization of the self.

Plato gave utmost importance to education. According to him education plays a vital role, which helps to serve the ruler, and it gives right direction to secure a harmonious state. Plato stated that if citizens are well educated they will be able to know the difficulties that surround them and find solutions.

In the Plato's *Republic* education has assumed great importance. In the words of Rousseau the Book of Plato's *Republic* was the greatest work on education ever written. [1]

Education is a continuous process which goes on whether school keeps or not. People learn any thing before they enter into the school followed by continuity outside the schoolroom. They keep on learning even if the formal education comes to an end.

Even during the hours of formal schooling, the students learn much outside, which doesn't constitute a part of the planned curriculum. The student secures a great deal of education from the church, political discussion and also from Magazines, Newspapers, Radio, and Television, which are employed 'as a means of educating'.

The word education is derived from the following Latin words:

1. Educare "The word conveys the meaning "To nourish", "To bring up", "To raise". This means to bring up the child or to nourish the child according to certain aims or ends in view.
2. Educere: - It means to "bring forth" or 'to lead'.
3. Educo: - It means "out of", "To lead out of." It also indicates to draw out everything from the child.
4. Educatum: - It is an act of teaching and training. This word may be treated as an external phenomenon. It is something imposed from the outside.

While the terms educare and educo may be understood in the context of right from within education is an external growth.

Scope of Education

Education in India as observed by Gandhi is completely out of touch both with the realities of national life and the upsurge of national aspirations. It is not related to the new forces that have been starring in the world. This type of education has given youth little insight in their national culture as it neither strengthens nor weakens.[2] Education is an all-round drawing out of the best in child and man—body, mind and spirit. Real education consists in drawing the best out of one self and there is no better book than the book of humanity.[3]

Gandhi holds that the ancient aphorism 'Education is that which liberates' is as true today as it was before. Education does not mean acquiring of mere spiritual knowledge and liberation does not signify spiritual liberation after death. Liberation means freedom from all manner of servitude.[4] Education to be imparted must be of new type for the sake of the creation of a new world.[5]

True education of the intellect according to Gandhi, comes through a proper exercise and training of the bodily organs such as hands, eyes, ears etc. An intelligent use of the bodily organs in a child provides the best and the quickest way to develop his intellect. Unless the development of the mind and body goes hand in hand with a corresponding awakening of the soul, the education would prove to be poor and lap sided. A proper and all-round development of the mind therefore can take place only when it proceeds equally the education of the physical and spiritual faculties of the child.[6]

Gandhi is a firm believer in the principle of free and compulsory primary education in India. Children need to have a useful vocational teaching and this has to be utilized as a means for cultivation of their mental, physical and spiritual faculties.[7] Gandhi holds that goodness is inherent in the soul of every individual but it needs to be drawn by the teachers. Such of those teachers whose own character is insulted, ready to learn and to grow from perfection to perfection can perform this sacred function.[8]

Education for Gandhi is a gift which distinguishes man from the beast. Gandhi does not agree with the view that the fullest development is impossible without a knowledge of the art of reading and writing. He considers this notion as superstitious. This knowledge however undoubtedly adds grace to life but it is in no way-indispensable for man's moral, physical or motional life.[9]

Gandhi does not believe in the existing system of education. He had a mind to find out by experience and experiment the true system. Gandhi regards character building as the proper foundation for their education. If the foundation is firmly laid, the children could learn all the other things themselves or with the assistance of friends.[10]

Gandhi arrives at the following conclusions for a number of years about education. He wishes to enforce when-ever he has the opportunity to enforce them.

Gandhi says:

1. "I am not opposed to education even of the highest type attainable in the world.
2. The state must pay for it whenever it has definite use for it.
3. I am opposed to all higher education being paid for from the general revenue.
4. It is my firm conviction that the vest amount of the so-called education in arts, given in our colleges is sheer waste and has resulted in unemployment among the educated classes. What is more, it has destroyed the health both mental and physical of the boys and girls who have the misfortune to go through the grind in our College.
5. The medium of a foreign language which higher education has been imparted in India has caused incalculable intellectual and moral injury to the nation. We are too near to our to judge the enormity of the damage done. And we who have received such

education have both to be victims and judges - an almost impossible feat.[11]

Gandhi holds that the universities must be made self-supporting. The state should simply educate such of those whose services are required. As far as the other branches of learning are concerned, it should encourage private effort. The medium of instruction should be given their rightful place. He opposes criminal waste in higher education. Gandhi does not claim to be an enemy of higher education but stands against the way in which it is given in our country. In his scheme of education/ there will be more and more better libraries, laboratories and Research Institutions under which there should be an army of chemists, engineers, and other experts who will become the real servants of the nation and answer the varied and growing requirements of the people who are conscious of their rights and needs. The knowledge gained by these experts will be for the common good of the people. The work will be original without any limitation.[12]

Process of Education

Education is a dynamic process that contributes to the natural harmonious development of individual powers, which are inherent and innate. It contributes to the complete human development resulting in the desirable behavioral change and ultimately prepares for a better life. Education is a process of development at different stages of human beings from infancy to the matured state. It is a process by where human being adopts himself gradually in various ways of use – physical, spiritual and environmental.

A newly born infant is a helpless human being. He has no knowledge of social customs and traditions. He does not have an idea to achieve an ideal or values. In the passage of time does she grow older with the influence of the informal and formal process of education. By this way he develops in the physical mental and emotional spheres and his feelings have also been developed gradually.

In due course he develops a sense of responsibility to find solutions to solve the problems and to deal with the problems confronted by him successfully. Education is an integral part of human life and it is a precondition for the development of the whole man.

It plays a vital role for the human being and achieves prosperity of all in very direction. In the absence of education man remains as beast or savage without any reason.

The word education has varied meanings; the meaning of education is complex in nature. It may be referred to formal schooling or to a lifelong education.

Each person interprets education depending on his personal interest and expectations of it. Education is considered to be a positive force enabling the child to prosper and to make progress. Teacher may interpret education as a means for the creation of a new man, the new society and for the emergence of a new Nation. For a student education is an acquisition of knowledge, attitudes and skills, and to get through examinations and receive degrees and diplomas.

The administration dealing with education believes education as a source of assistance and support to secure pass in the examination whereas an artisan thinks education as a means to achieve mastery over a skill. In the case of a religious teacher education is a method to abolish ignorance dispel darkness and instill spiritual values in the minds of the people. For a statesman, education is a means to train the people as good ideal citizens.

Man is distinguishable primarily from the lower cadre of animals. He is endowed with intelligence, understanding educative ability.

The word education has varied meanings. It is difficult to give precise meaning and definition. The definition of education for a biologist is different from a psychologist a states man and sociologist. They give different definition.

Etymological Meaning of Education

The word education is derived from the Latin word *educare*, which means 'to bring up'. There is another word 'educare' which means to bring forth. So the meaning of the word education means both to bring forth the as well as to bring up. Varro stated that education means "the mid-wife brings forth, the nurse brings up; the tutor trains, and the master teaches."[13] So education means the development of habits, attitudes and skills, which help a man to lead a full and worthwhile life but not merely the acquition of knowledge and experiences. Education is the act or process of educating or being educated with systematic instruction. Education on the other hand contributes to the development of character and mental powers.

Education Modifiles the Human Behaviour

Education is an activity or a process, which transforms the behaviour of a person from instinctive behaviour to human behavior. Man instead of acting impulsively acts rationally. Education gives a new shape to man. John Ruskin stated that it is not to educate a man by telling him what the knows not but by making him what he was not.

Education in a Process of Training

Education has a purpose to train the children to train the children to fulfil the responsibilities of adult life children have to become responsible citizens and discharge their duties as members of the society when they become adults. Education gives them right direction. Education develops proper thinking and reasoning when they grow. An individual needs training to use his own reasoning to enable them to lead an orderly and moral life.

True education means training the individual, which enables him to distinguish between good and evil. Education is the training for the intellect, body and spirit.

Gandhi defines education in the following words:

> By education I mean an all-round drawing out of the best in the child and man—body and spirit. Literacy is not the end of education or even the beginning. It is only one of the means where by man and woman can be educated.[14]

The nature of educational philosophy varies from one country to the other. In Germany, which was under the rule of a dictator, has different educational philosophy. The policies of the dictator have been reflected in the educational philosophy of Germany. In the democratic countries like India and Great Britain there is one type of educational philosophy whereas in the communist countries like Russia and China, there has been different type of educational philosophy. In the countries ruled by Dictators the policies and rules will be dictated by the government. The government decides the nature and type of the curriculum and syllabi. Others are not empowered to restructure the syllabi or bring about educational reforms. In the democratic countries students and teachers enjoy a great amount of freedom.

They can propose reforms and changes in education. In the communistic countries, the principles of Communism, Marxism have been taught.[15]

When education is seen as a whole, it is found to be useful, critical and a systematic intellectual endeavour. It is an integral part of man's culture.[16]

Education as Process of Growth

The child grows as he learns day by day. In the words of John Dewey education is a continuous process of adjustment with an added capacity of growth. It is the bounded duty of the teacher to provide opportunities for proper growth by arousing the instincts and capacities of the child. The teacher also has to make the child think about the problem and the solution of the problem, which enables the child to think about. When the child is made to think the power of thinking grows. His mind also grows. Thereby child develops more capacity, for further thoughts. An individual is a changing and growing personality says John Dewey. The purpose of education is to facilitate the process of his growth.

Education and the process of learning are inter-connected. While all experience results in learning, all learning is a product of experience and development is due to learning. The process of growth and development caused by learning depending on experience is called Education. Education is the reconstruction of these experiences.

In the creation of God, human life assumes more significance and it is the most sacred. The human life is marked by two main important aspects. They are biological and sociological aspects. The biological aspect of human life is maintained as transmitted by nutrition and reproduction. The sociological aspects of human life is maintained and transmitted by education. In the antiquity, the basic needs of the people living in the early society were limited to food, clothing and shelter. In the passage of time, the society emulated civilized conduct of life and the human needs became multiplied viz., food, clothing, shelter education, recreation and health. Man is distinguished from an animal because of education imparted to him.

In order to learn how to do some thing, the students acquire skills. They learn that some thing is the case, they acquire the related information. They learn what ought to be the case imbued with values. A successful student learns how to meet the demands of the school even though most of the skills needed for this purpose are not transferable to the non-school situations. The students learn disposition not programmed by the school, which include attitudes towards learning, towards participation in cultural events and towards the degree of involvement necessary by superiors. These contents of learning must be included with in the meaning of education.

Training is considered to be a kind of education, which is some thing not different from it. Training is education leading to learning how to do some thing to the learning of skills. It is job-oriented. It cannot be branded as inferior to other kinds of learning. A great part of the preparation to achieve professional expertise in the field of medicine, law and engineering consisting of learning skills. The greater part of all vocational preparation is skill training.

Education does not stop at the end of formal schooling. Education is not limited to the premises of an established school. On the other hand, it is not limited in time to a particular period of a learner pursuing studies.

Although education plays a vital role in the human life and education has become a primary concern of the nation, there is range or limitation to educational interests and practices. Education undergoes changes continuously. Education is viewed as institution, as process and as a product.

Education is considered to be a process, clearly concerned with learning and teaching but it is not the end of the process. If we examine education from different standpoints we find the sociologists viewing the public schools as a process of social control whereas the political scientists view them as process by which the state instills values essential to its survival. The economists and a large number of citizens view schooling as a process by which young people are equipped to enter into the useful work force. Education as a process is concerned not merely with the ends of instruction and the means by which the people have attained their objective but also appropriately what they have learned as well.[17]

The child is adaptable. He could learn to behave in almost any way. The human beings who constitute an important part of the environment in which he lives in, behaves in comparatively fixed and highly in a standardized way. For instance a child has not developed the food taste. He could learn to like meat, fish and vegetables. He is born amidst of the persons, of the persons, along with whom he lives. He has very limited and stable food habits. He can be bended. The environment is rigid. The human being adjusts himself to his environment through the years of his infancy, child hood and youth this can be termed as education.

When viewed from this perspective, education becomes co-extensive with life. Every stage of experience in life, big or small is educative. It affects the personality and modifies the human behavior People consciously or unconsciously are being educated in every walk of their life. Thus life becomes synonymous with the act of living. So education need not be necessarily connected with schools or colleges alone.

According to John Dewey, education must be based on experience and education must be applied to experience also If life means growth and if education becomes necessary and contributes to the full and continued growth of human beings, education cannot be excluded to adult life or to attain some narrow vocation. When education is taken in the good sense and the evil sense continues for an entire lifetime. So education is to know how it will offer its better services and continue to serve all processes of living that contribute to their widest possible growth. There have been wider possibilities for growth and it is unlimited and inevitable. The growth of education must necessarily be on the right lines. It must be directed towards a desirable end without any reference to the predetermined goals and ends. The end of growth is more growth and the end of education is to achieve better and more education.

Gandhian Philosophy of Education

Philosophy is varied in meaning and in scope. The word Philo means love or fond of and Sophia means wisdom. Thus Philosophy means love of wisdom or pursuit of knowledge. Plato used the term in a general way in his book '*The Republic*'. He applied it to those who see the absolute, eternal and immutable and also to those who love the truth in each thing.

The philosophy of education has undergone and continues to undergo some profound changes. In the past an author could discuss the philosophy of education with reference to the idealists and pragmatists. Although there is need for extending the boundaries of philosophy of education, the appearances of the problems associated with the philosophy of education are sporadic.

The *Encyclopedia of Philosophy of Education* defines education in the following words:

> The philosophy of education may be either the philosophy of the process of education or the philosophy of the process of education or the philosophy of the discipline of education. That is, it may be part of the discipline in the sense of being concerned with the aims, forms, methods or results of educating or being educated or it may be inter meta disciplinary in the sense of being concerned with the concepts, aims and methods of the discipline.[18]

In the modern times there have been some philosophers who reject all metaphysical statements completely as nonsense for they believe the statements as unverifiable but they are more likely to think of ethical statements as imperative.

In the twentieth century philosophy of education tended to be developed in schools of education in the context of what is known as foundations of education linking with other parts of the discipline of education namely educational history, psychology sociology rather than with other aspects of philosophy.

Philosophy of education has been defined as an attempt to find answers to questions, which are termed as ultimate. A philosopher dealing with education is desirous of learning what is knowable and what he has to do with education. He is interested in the nature of reality, sources of value and the aspects such as aims, curriculum and method may mean for education.

He may or may not believe that he is capable of knowing the nature of ultimate reality and the values are discovered by intuition or revelation. He may reduce or may not reduce all knowledge to observation and experimentation. But his views on metaphysics, epistemology and axiology are connected with their implications of education. What philosophy of education to one philosopher is different from the philosophy of education of another for the reason that their ideas and line of thinking vary.

Philosophy of education helps to think clearly, carefully, rigorously and systematically relating to educational problems and concepts. It is clarifying and liberating.

It tends to make people to be more conscious of important issues helping them to evaluate. It serves to free them from the tyranny of conventional thought. When the philosophy of education fails to perform to achieve the desirable ends expected of, it merely remains as an intellectual exercise.[19]

Philosophy has been defined in ways implying a certain totality, generality, and ultimateness of both subject matter and method. With regard to subject matter philosophy is an attempt to comprehend which is to gather the varied details of the world and of life into a single inclusive whole which shall either be a unity or as in the dualistic systems shall reduce the plural details to a small number of ultimate principles, on the side of the attitude of the philosopher and of those who accept his conclusions, there is the endeavor to attain as unified and complete an out look upon experience as possible. This word is expressed in the word. Philosophy, which means love of wisdom. When philosophy is taken into consideration, it is assumed that it signifies the acquisition of knowledge, which influences the conduct of life. [20]

John Dewey observes that

> Philosophy of education is not an external application of ready made ideas to a system of practice having a radically different origin and purpose; it is only an explicit formulation of the problems of the formation of right mental and moral habitudes in respect of the difficulties of contemporary social life.[21]

Application of method in educational activity assumes great importance as it not only evaluates the founded tradition of the past but also enhances the capacity; to enrich it.[22] Education fascinates the citizen and the scholar in the same manner in the modern era as it assumes great importance. The new and expanding economic political and social functions pull education into the main stream of society.

Theodore Brameld holds that there has been crisis in education as well as in culture. Education is part and parcel of culture. It follows that a crisis philosophy of education must presuppose a crisis philosophy of culture.

Mankind is living in atomic age capable of destroying over night, and also producing a higher level of civilization on world scale than man has ever known. People are at the crossroads. One way leads to wards destruction and the other towards reconstruction. [23]

Brameld holds that the reconstructionist is very clear about the way the mankind should take. They have to make a choice Education gives right direction and enables them to choose the way of reconstruction.[24]

If we observe we find the world, which has been split, into warring camps that expend much of their energy and resources in hating each other and trying to destroy each other. Hate and destruction re disvalues which seem to have been conspicuous in the human life than the values of love co-operation and construction. So there is need to reconstructionists to promote peace. [25]

Function of Education

There is need to think about the meaning functions and aims of education. There are interconnected, interrelated and closely inter woven.

Education enables the child to think for himself to give regard work, to have good fellowship to develop taste and sense of eternal realities. The purpose of education is to discover aptitudes and to train them to be of social use. Education enables a person to make a choice of values. Education makes a distinction between the desirable and the undesirable and enables an individual to choose the desirable. Selection of desirable from the undesirable requires knowledge and insight, which could be achieved through the right type of education. Education must necessarily make the pupil to suit the environment.

Education is a social process and it is possible in a social environment. In the modern days the concept of education as a social function has not changed. The methods to be followed have changed. In the modern times the society unlike in the primitive days is complex. So it was very simple for the society to transmit its experiences to the new generation. The society to day being very complex cannot transmit its knowledge and skills to the rising generation.

The need for the establishment of schools is felt in order to impart essential knowledge and fundamental skills in an organized manner. However the establishment of school does not prevent the role of other educational agencies like church, home. TV, radio, press and other influences of the environment. But the school is a selected and a controlled environment.

The Aims of Education

The human society owes its existence because of education. There is need to know about the goals, aims or objectives of education. Without determining the aims of education, it is not possible to plan the curriculum and the methods to be followed to impart that curriculum. Aim enables to act with a purpose and meaning. Education gives right direction to that activity. In the absence of the aims in education, progress cannot be achieved. A study of the history of education reveals that hundreds of aims have been given at different times and different places by the different thinkers of education. No two persons think alike since their psychic structure varies.

Similarly no two persons express the aims of education precisely in the same way. Manu, the ancient law-giver states that the aim of education is to achieve intellectual and spiritual development. For Plato the aim of education was to allow the individual to develop along the line of his own powers. According to the Aryans of the ancient times in India, spiritualism was the main aim education. For Spartans the aim of their education was the preparation for a life of military duties. They laid more stress on the physical prowess, courage, discipline and obedience. A marked difference could be noticed while Spartans cared more for body than for the mind; the Athenians wanted a harmonious blend of body and mind to achieve progress and development.

In an ideal society the aims of education is determined by higher ideals of life. In this society the aims looked at are ultimate and general but not specific. It is meant for the general development of a person. The education imparted is to build character, for individual and social development

For the promotion of culture, mental discipline acquisition of knowledge for knowledge sake and so on. The approach of education is idealistic and all these are partial ideals.

Taking the existing state of society into consideration comes under the realistic way of approaching education. The existing philosophy of life, the prevailing political ideologies, the existing social problems and economic conditions determine the aims of education. The prevailing philosophical out look reflects on the aims of education.

Plato attached great importance to education. Education plays a vital role in the human life. It is through education that a ruler can shape the human nature in the right direction in order to produce a harmonious state. When knowledge is taught as a virtue; the educational system becomes an indispensable part of a good state. According to Plato with a good system of education any improvement is possible. When education is neglected, other matters also become neglected and progress will be lopsided. The education has to be provided in consonance with the harmonious and well-being of the state.

So Plato aims at the state controlled compulsory education. His scheme of education can be categorized under two parts, the elementary education inclusive of training for young persons up to the age of twenty culminating in the beginning of military service and the higher education intended for the selected persons of both sexes who are the members of the ruling classes between the age of twenty and thirty five. The state directed scheme of education, which is compulsory, is an important innovation of Athemian practice.

The aim of education is to enable individuals to continue their education. The object and reward of learning is continued capacity for growth.

John Dewey states that

> An aim denotes the result of any natural process brought

> to consciousness and made a factor in determining present observation and choice of ways of acting. It signifies that an activity has become intelligent. Specifically it means foresight of the alternative consequence as attendant upon acting in a given situation in different ways and the use of what is anticipated to direct observation and experiment. A true aim is thus opposed at every point to an aim, which is imposed upon a process of action from without.[26]

Education gives Right Direction

Educating a child means to give right and proper direction to the child. The prime concern of the education is to direct the undeveloped capacities, attitudes, interests urges and needs of the young people into to the most desirable channels. Children have been born with instincts. They have to be properly directed so that their satisfaction may be socially acceptable. Educative process involves to direct the children to have worthy interests in various phases of life. Education creates environment conducive for stimulation to develop desirable attributes of individual and social personality.

Direction followed by wisdom includes guidance and control. Guidance is an essential aspect to have a proper stimulus to be given for arousing correct responses in the child. Control is needed to have a check on the antisocial impulses of the child. The child has to be kept away from the selfish and antisocial tendencies. Control helps in the elimination of unnecessary movements on the part of the child.

Education as direction envisages the impact on persons and things. Persons influence the children directly and indirectly. It can be pointed out that education is a wise direction. In the process of direction both the direct way and the indirect way is stated to be useful. While the poor direction results in egocentric personality, proper and careful direction produces socially responsive personality.

Education as Integral Growth

Man undergoes many changes in his lifetime. These changes are physical, emotional and mental. When the changes are obvious, there occurs growth. Growth is conditioned by two factors. Training and Environment. Every person acts, reacts and interacts as his environment. The training he undergoes makes him capable. Man through training makes him grow. Growing is education and receiving education is growing.

Human life has many habits, which are good, bad and indifferent in nature. There efforts of education result in the formation of good habits. It is essential that people must learn to cultivate moral, intellectual and emotional habits.

In the recent past, the emphasis of education has shifted to the social development side and child's civic efficiency. Hitherto education has catered for the segment of student's whole personality but it has not catered to balanced and integrated growth of the child. It is only when all the dimensions of the child-physical, spiritual and moral, intellectual, social and aesthetic are harmoniously blended, that state is called the integrated growth of the child. The report of the Mudaliar Commission constituted during 1952-53 states that:

> "The training of character to fit the students to participate creatively as citizens in the emerging democratic social order; the improvements of their practical and vocational efficiency so that they may play their part in building up the economic prosperity of their country; and the development of their literary artistic and cultural interests which are necessary for self-expression and for the full development of the human personality, without which a living national culture can not come into being".[27]

Integrated growth should be an all-round growth. The pupil should and feel that his destiny is in his hands. The kind of person he wants to become depends on his own decision. Children must be directed towards some thing worthwhile in their personal and social relations. They must grow up to be something admirable models and patterns. Growth has to be towards an ideal of human character. Growth on right lines leads to an adequacy and contended life.

Education is a continuous process Education is growth when education implies growth, it does not stop. It is a continuous process through out life. Education does not end with the school life. It continues even after the school Education is not confined to any period of time. It is for the whole life. When education in its process of growth, progress or development, it becomes a vital force. It conserves the cultural values of the past and transmits to the succeeding generation. Education creates conditions conducive for the progress of man.

The environments undergo changes. Individuals have to change as per the changed conditions. The new generations have been confronted with new situations.

The transmitted knowledge of experience and activities have to be organized in order to meet the new challenges and situations. An integration of old with the new, makes the human life more dynamic and progressive. Education helps a person to avoid the social evils, which might have crept the society in the process of time.

Education is the formation of mind by the selection and co-ordination of the inherent abilities and capabilities in the manner by which they may utilize the matter relating to the social environment.

According to John Dewey education is the unfolding of the latent powers and the formation of mind depending on the physical nature or by the cultural products of the past, which result in a constant reorganization, and reconstruction of experiences.

Education is the reconstruction or reorganization of experience. Education adds to the meaning of experience. The first experience of a child becomes meaning full. The child begins to perceive the connection of heat with other things. Thereby the child's mind stands educated or instructed. The child becomes of aware of interconnections in education. His mental horizon is widened. The child does not learn from the experience he gets and reconstructs one mode of activity of thinking alone. But he gets education from many experiences. The process of educative experiences draws him to the conception of education as continuous reconstruction.

It may be added that every continuous experience or activity is educative. Education promotes to have such experience. Education as a constructive agency, improves the human society.

Education exerts profound influence on all the aspects of the human endeavor. The human character and faculties are influenced by various factors- the social life, the church, the political life, the form of government, the natural environment, the radio, the press the hobbies, the travels, the educational institutions etc. All these are agencies of education apart from the schools, all other are agencies of education representing the informal education.

All the informal agencies of education exert great influence in the matter of shaping the personality of the child. Their teaching is indirect and incidental. For instance the home unconsciously helps the child to learn the language, modes of behavior and attitudes towards different intuitions of society. The church sets up the standards of the individual to the higher moral values of life. The government, the radio; the press etc. are potentially strong in the context of education provided their objectives are in conformity with the truths of life.

Education is not confined to the mere classroom or a school alone. It is not limited to a specific period of life. Education is a life long process, which goes on from cradle to the grave.

Mahatma Gandhi and Education

Character building has first place in Gandhian education. Character is similar to foundation. A building built on sand collapses where as a building erected on a strong foundation lasts for long time. Gandhi holds that the school must be an extension of home. There must be agreement between the impressions, which a child gathers at home and at school to achieve the best results. The alien type of education produces a gulf between the educated classes and the masses.[28]

Gandhi does not think it necessary to consider whether the adoption of the mother tongue as the medium of instruction would have any adverse effect on the knowledge of English or not. It is necessary of the foreign language. He further states that it is unnecessary to create and encourage a liking for it.

Gandhi states that English cannot and ought not to become the National language. In this connection Gandhi refers to the requirement of a national language.

He says that

1. It should be easy to learn for government officials.
2. It should be capable of serving as medium of religious, economic and political intercourse through out India.
3. It should be the speech of the majority of the inhabitants of India.
4. Every body should find it easy to learn.

5. In choosing such a language considerations of temporary or passing interest should not count. [29]

Gandhi states that English language does not fulfill any of these requirements. To think that English language can become Indian national language is a sign of weakness.

Gandhi stated that the teachers teaching have to lead an exemplary life with high moral character. Conditions have to be created so as to enable the poorest Indian to receive the best possible education. There must be a union of literary knowledge and *dharma*. The type of education imported to the people must necessarily be related to the conditions of life in India. Imposing heavy burden on the minds of young people resulting from the use of a foreign language, as the medium of instruction must be removed. There is need to reshape and redesign education in order to raise the level of the people. True natural education should be imparted through the language followed by each province. The teachers imparting education must be men of high ability. The surroundings of the school have to be clean healthy and conducive to promote good education with basic amenities such as good drinking water, pure air and peaceful atmosphere.

The scheme of education must provide knowledge so as to secure the main occupations and religions with good understanding of the country.

Gandhi felt the need to overhaul education system. He thought of National education and proposed the following methods to be evolved.

1. Education must be imparted through the mother tongue
2. There must be accord between the education a child receives at the school and the environment of the home

3. It must be so planned as to meet the needs of the majority of the people.
4. The teachers in primary classes must be competent of good character right from the first class.
5. Education must be free
6. Over all control must be in the hands of the people.[30]

Mother Tongue

Education must be imparted through mother tongue. People have been lured by English language. Those who advocate English language state that it is through English that an awakening has been created in the country. English literature is vast and widely used. Giving up the use of English is a misfortune. It is not possible to translate it into other languages. Unity could be achieved only through English. Encouragement for the promotion of different languages of India is tantamount to disrupt the unity and retard the growing feeling of unity that they are of one nation. These are the main arguments of the advocates of English.

Education should not be made dependent on money. As the sun gives light to all the rich and the poor and rain falls on all so also learning must be made available to all.[31]

Education and Science

The fact that education places an exclusive emphasis on literary merit is found to be a defect. Gandhi finds that while pursuing literary studies, students do not render service at the sacrifice of their service. He holds that the students do not lose any thing or gain much if they suspend their literary or industrial education to attend to relief work.

Gandhi says that

> The end of all education should surely be service and if a student gets an opportunity of rendering service even whilst he is studying, he should consider it as a rare

opportunity and treat it not really as a suspension of his education but rather to complement.[32]

Building of Character

Gandhi states that learning has value but the development of good character is more important than learning.

For Gandhi religion means truth and ahimsa. Ahimsa is the means and truth is the end. Truth is inclusive of *ahimsa*. Ahimsa is the indispensable means for the discovery of truth. Anything that promotes the practice of the virtues – Truth and *ahimsa* is a means for imparting religious education. It is when the teachers imparting religious education rigorously practice these virtues could promote and practice of these virtues.

Gandhi holds that a curriculum of religious instruction should include a study of the tenets of faiths apart from their own. The students have to be trained in such a manner so as to cultivate the habit of understanding and appreciating the doctrines of various great religions of the world in a spirit of reverence and broad-minded tolerance.[33]

Gandhi states that the study of other religious besides one's own gives a grasp of the rock bottom unity of all religions. This study could afford a glimpse also of that universal and absolute. Truth which lies beyond the 'Dust of creeds and faiths'.[34]

On the other hand Gandhi does not believe that the state can concern itself or cope with religious education. He states that religious education must be the sole concern of religious associations. He does not like the idea of mixing up religion with ethics for the reason all the fundamental ethics is common to all religions. So teaching of fundamental ethics is undoubtedly a function of the state.[35] In the even that the government feels the need of the religious instruction to be included in education, it is imperative that the religious instruction offered should be of the best type; says Gandhi.[36] The aim of all religious teaching has to make men more tolerant and broad minded.

Education Imparted in the Tolstoy Farm

Gandhi did not believe in the existing system of education. He had a mind to experiment the true system of education. He held that the true system of education could be imparted only by the parents. Tolstoy Farm was a family in which Gandhi occupied the place of the father. He has to shoulder the responsibility for the training of the young.

Gandhi has given priority to the culture of the heart or building of the character. He strongly believed that moral training could be given to all alike irrespective of their age difference. Gandhi decided to live amongst them throughout the day as their father. He regarded character building as the proper foundation for their education. He held that when the foundation is firmly laid, the children could learn all other things themselves or with the co-operation of their friends.

He appreciated the necessity of a literary training also. The students became adapt to the course of their daily routine. Since there were no servants on the Farm, all the work from cooking, scavenging etc. was done by the inmates. Added to it there were many fruit trees to be looked after and enough gardening work to be attended to. It was obligatory on all young and old who did not engage in the kitchen to spare sometime to attend to gardening. The children had the lion's share of this work, which included digging pits felling limer and lifting loads. This gave them ample exercise. They took delight in the work. There was scarcely any illness on the Farm because of good maintenance.

One of the inmates learnt shoe making and Gandhi learnt it from him. He taught the art to enable the inmates to be ready to take it up. Some of them know carpentry also. They had classes to learn carpentry.

In the Tolstoy Farm they made it a policy that the youngsters should not be asked to do what the teachers did not do. Whenever the youngsters do any work, there was always a teacher co-operating and actually working with them. So what even the youngsters learnt, they learnt cheerfully.

In the morning, Gandhi used to devote his time to work on the Farm and to attend to domestic duties. School hours were kept after the mid day meal for there was no other suitable time for the school. Three hours were allotted to the literary training Hindi, Tamil, Gujarati and Urdu were all taught as well. Tuition was given through the vernaculars of the boys. English was also taught.

The love Gandhi had for the languages of India, his confidence in his capacity as a teacher, and the ignorance of his pupils and their generously stood with him in good stead. He did not feel the need for the use of the textbooks. He could never member to have used the textbooks that were available. More over he did not feel the need to load the boys with quantities of books. He was of the opinion that the true textbook for the textbook for the pupil is his teacher. He remembers very little that the teachers taught him from books but he has had a clear recollection of the things they taught him independently of books.

Gandhi holds that children take in much more and with less labor through their ears than through their eyes. He did not remember to have read any book from page to page along with his boys. But he taught using his own language all that he digested through the study of various books. The pupils could carry a recollection of it in their minds. It was laborious for them to remember what they learnt from books but what was imparted to them through mouth they could repeat without any difficulty with ease.

Gandhi found that the spiritual training to be much more difficult matter than their physical and mental training. He believed that every student should be acquainted with the elements of his own religion and also with a general knowledge of his own scriptures. He realized that the training of the spirit was a thing by itself. It is by building character and by working to get knowledge of God and self-realization one could develop the spirit. He found it to be the essential part of the young. All training without culture of the spirit was of no use and might prove harmful.

Spiritual training could be given by making the children memorize and recite hymns and read to them from books on moral training. Gandhi could realize that no one could impart training of the spirit through books. Just as physical training was to be imparted through physical exercise and intellectual through intellectual exercise so also the training of the spirit was possible only through the exercise of the spirit. The exercise of the spirit depends entirely upon the life and character of the teacher. He has to stand as a good model to the students. Gandhi imposed the increasing discipline and restraint on himself at Tolstoy Farm to be a good model.

Gandhi held that delinquency on the part of the pupil's call for even the drastic remedy of fasting by the teacher on some occasions. It presupposes clearness of vision and spiritual fitness. Gandhi's says that "where there is no true love between the teacher and the pupil, where the pupil's delinquency has not touched the very being of the teacher and where the pupil has no respect for the teacher, fasting is out of place and even be harmful". [37] There is possibility for doubting the propriety of fasts in some cases but the question of teacher's responsibilities does not arise.

New Education, and Culture of the People

The curriculum and pedagogic ideas were constituted from the fabric of modern education. They were imported from oxford and Cambridge, Edinburgh and London. They are essentially foreign. Unless they are repudiated, national education cannot be offered.

Gandhi holds that the fact to be realized is that India by the very fact of her long established and elaborated civilization which has had the advantage of an educational system of her own called 'national'. It was fundamentally distinct from the Anglo-Indian type and from the psedo-national type, which is its descendant. The choice has to be made between national and foreign education. So long as confusion exists on this matter, education can not flourish.

Gandhi pointed out that the greatest visible evil present in the educational method is the defect, which has broken its continuity of human existence. The sound education has to fit in one generation to take up the burden of the provisions and to keep up the life of the community without any breach or disaster. The burden of social life is continuous In any event if one generation gets completely out of touch with the efforts of its predecessors or other wise gets ashamed of itself or its culture. Gandhi stated that the force that maintains society to gather is a series of high loyalties- loyalty to faith parents, family; dharma etc. The ancient system of education in India maintained the long tradition imbued with values, pride and service, the place of every order with in the body social and body polite.

Gandhi holds that the system of education offered in the modern world has no connection with the surroundings. They remain practically untouched by the education received by a microscopic minority of boys and girls of the nation.

The English teacher could not wholly understand the difference between English and Indian requirements. The children brought up with rural environment need no urban-based surroundings and the type of education offered to the English children.

Gandhi pointed out that his scheme of education does not exclude literary training. No course of primary instruction will be complete which did not include reading, writing and arithmetic.

Integrated Education

Gandhi held that true education of the intellect can come through a proper exercise and training of the bodily organs e.g. hands, feet, eyes ears, nose etc. It is by the intelligent use of the bodily organs by the child that provides the best and quickest way to develop the intellect of the child. The development of the mind and body should go hand in hand with a corres ponding awakening of the soul. Or else the development of the mind will prove poor and lopsided affair. A proper and all round development of the mind therefore can take place only when it proceeds on equal speed with the education of the physical and spiritual faculties of the child. They're indivisible whole. It would be a gross fallacy to suppose that they can be developed piece meal or independent of one another.

In the absence of proper co-ordination and harmony among the various faculties of body, mind and soul the effects are baneful, says Gandhi. When the child is set to some useful occupation like spinning, carpentry agriculture etc. for his education and is given a thorough comprehensive knowledge relating to the theory of the various operations, that he is to perform and the use and construction of the tools that he wields. There by he develops a fine, healthy body and also a sound, vigorous intellect His intellectual education includes knowledge of mathematics and the various sciences that are useful for an intelligent and efficient exercise of his occupation. The study of literature gives him a perfect well balanced all round education in which the intellect, body and the spirit have all full play. This develops together into a natural and a harmonious whole. Man is not mere intellect alone. Hs is not the gross animal body. He is not the heart or soul alone. He is a proper and harmonious combination of all the three, which is required for the making of the whole man. It constitutes the true economies of education, says Gandhi.

Wardha Scheme of Education

Gandhi spoke strongly in the year 1920 against the existing system of education, which has got the opportunity to influence the ministers in the seven provinces. They were fellow workers in the struggle for freedom of the country. Gandhi held that in Educational Reconstruction that to make good the charge that the present mode of education is radically wrong from top to bottom. While writing a series of articles regarding his ideals and ideas on educational reconstruction in India; he suggested a scheme of universal compulsory education for all children between the age group of 13 –15 through the medium of mother tongue, which would be self-supporting that leads to all round development of the pupils. The industrial vocations such a the processing of cotton, wool and silk paper making and cutting book binding, cabinet making etc taught at the primary schools should serve a double purpose. They should help the pupils to pay for their tuition through the products of their labors while developing them through the vacations learnt at these schools.

Wardha Conference

The ideas of Gandhi on self-supporting aspect of the scheme described as basic education published in the Harijan resulted in a great public stir. It is called basic since it is expected to constitute the basis of national culture. It was thought desirable to get the scheme examined by export educationists. With that end in view the First Conference on National Education was called at Wardha on 22nd & 23rd Oct 1937 with Gandhi in the chair. The conference was attended by the Education Ministers of the seven Provinces with the congress Ministers. The number of delegates was limited to national workers particularly workers in national education. Gandhi personally placed his scheme of national education through rural handicrafts before the conference. After a serious discussion the following resolutions were adopted:

1. That in the opinion of this conference free and compulsory education be provided for seven years one on a nationwide scale.
2. That the medium of instruction be the mother tongue.
3. That the conference endorses the proposal made by Mahatma Gandhi that the process of education through out this period should center round some form of manual productive work and that all the other abilities to be developed or training to be given should as far as possible; be integrally related to the central handicraft chosen with due regard to the environment of the child.
4. That the conference expects that this system of education will be gradually able to cover the remuneration of teachers. [38]

This conference appointed a committee of educationists under the chairmanship of Dr. Zakin Husain to work out the details of the curriculum. The report received from the committee in the year 1938 was placed before the Indian National Congress the same year, which was accepted. The first Basic School was established at Sevagram near Wardha in 1938 under the supervision of Mahatma Gandhi. But the congress leaders and the Industrialists who represented the congress party showed great reluctance in moving from the existing colonially derived education system to Basic Education which lays stress on vocation and condemned it as child labour. They offered broad based curriculum instead for elementary education and expansion of facilities for technical education.[39]

Basic Education and Gandhi

Mahatma Gandhi stood for the educational system, which is literary and productive, But the existing system of education is completely separated from the life activities of the child with moral degradation. In order to abolish the evils that have beset the society and to achieve the ideal society economically self reliant peaceful and orderly and to uphold moral and spiritual life and to reduce the disparities and inequalities in the society he put for ward a new scheme of education known as basic education which has its basis on morality and human values. The following are the outlines of the fundamentals of Gandhian educational scheme.

All education to be true must be self-supporting

All education must be imparted through the medium of the provincial languages. In this there is no room for giving sectional religious training. Fundamental universal ethics will have full scope.

> This education whether confined to children or adults males or females will find its way to the homes of the pupils. Must learn an inter-provincial language. This language can only be Hindustani written in Nagari or Urdu script.[40]

Gandhi's basic idea was to make education self-supporting through craft, agriculture and other productive work there by by-passing potentially the need for government funding support.[41]

A committee constituted by educationists was headed by Dr. Zakir Husain in order to workout the details of the curriculum. The report of the committee received in the year 1938 was placed before Indian National Congress, which was accepted. The first basic school was established at Sevagram near Wardha in 1938 under Gandhi's personal supervision but the proposal of basic education was opposed by Congress leaders and industrialists. They showed great reluctance in moving from colonially derived system of basic education. They objected to the emphasis on vocation condemning it as child labour. Instead they offered broad based curriculum for elementary education and expansion of facilities for technical education.[42]

The system of basic education proposed by Gandhi leads to the development of the mind, body and soul whereas the ordinary system of education cares only for the mind.[43]

Literacy for him is not the end of education and it is not even the beginning of education. It is only a means to educate the people but literacy is not education. Gandhi wishes that child's education should begin with the teaching of a useful handicraft. This enables the child to produce from the moment the child begins his training. This helps every school to be self-supporting. Under such system of education, the highest envelopment of mind and soul becomes possible. Every handicraft needs to be taught not in a mechanical manner alone but scientifically. The child has to be in a position to know every process of it. The proposal introduced by Gandhi is of revolutionary type, which saves immense labor. It is economical on the other hand.[44]

Gandhi holds that an intellect which is developed through the medium of socially useful labor will be an instrument for service and it will not easily be led astray or fall into devious path.[45]

Gandhi looks upon education as an integral whole and also as an instrument of social revolution lifting the human life continually to something better culturally, socially, morally and spiritually.

Gandhi has named his educational programme as *Nai Talim*, which implies new education under which education has become life centered, instead of textbook centered. Nai Talim has been defined as education for life, through life and through out life. *Nai Talim* has been divided into pre-basic, basic, post-basic, university and social education. Pre-basic is the nursery school part, basic is elementary education for a period of eight years, between 7 and 15 years of age. Post-basic is High school education and social education has become adult education.[46]

Gandhi has taken up basic education for boys and girls between 7 and 15 years of age for a period of 8 years. In the view of Gandhi basic education is the birth right of every child in India. No child could remain without it if Indian humanity is to make progress.[47]

Basic education or *Nai Talim* (new system of education) as Gandhi calls it is revolutionary in its conception. It is based on the theory that it is the activity known s 'the thinking hand' which more than anything else has guided the evolution of man and society. In this system of whole education, man can be imparted through the medium of a basic handicraft. It's goal is to build up 'a non-violent, non-exploiting social order in which the ideals of freedom, equality, and brotherhood can be fully and universally realized.[48] This type of education is life centered but not textbook centered.[49]

Gandhi holds that craft, art, health and education should all be integrated into one scheme. Nai Talim is a beautiful blend of all the four and covers the whole education of the individual from the time of conception to the moment of death. He regards craft and industry as the medium of education.[50] He is of the opinion that if right kind of teachers are given, children will be taught the dignity of labor and learn to regard it as an integral part and as a means of their intellectual growth. He mainly suggests that handicrafts are to be taught not merely for productive work but for developing the intellect of the pupils. This helps them to be self-supporting.[51]

Education is popularly and correctly described as education through handicrafts but it is part by true. The root of the new education goes much deeper. It lies in the application of truth and love in every human activity. The notion of education through handicrafts rises from the contemplation of truth and love, which permeates every activity of the human life. True education should be made easily accessible to all. It should be of much use to every villager in his daily life. Such type of education does not depend on books.[52] The teacher's earning in this new education stands as the art of living. Therefore, both the teacher and the taught have to produce in the very act of teaching and learning, which enriches life from the very beginning.[53]

If we wish to impart education best suited to the needs of the villagers, we should take the vidyapith (seat of learning) to the villages and *vidyapith* has to be converted into a training school so that practical training, which suits the needs of the villagers, might be imparted. It does not hold good if the teachers are instructed to give training through a training school in a city as per the needs of villagers.

Gandhi is of the opinion that the commencement of training by teaching the alphabet and writing hampers the intellectual growth of the pupils. He proposes on the other hand to teach the alphabet when the pupils acquire elementary knowledge of history, geography and the art of spinning. Through these their intelligence should be developed.

> "Questions may be asked" says Gandhi, "how intelligence can be developed through *takli* or the spinning wheel. It can to a marvelous degree if it is not taught mere mechanically. When you tell child the reason for each process, when you explain the mechanism of the *takli* or the wheel, when you give him the history of cotton and its connection with civilization itself and take him to the village field where it is grown, and teach him to count the rounds he spins

> and the method of finding the evenness ands strength of his yarn, you hold his interest and simultaneously train his hands, his eyes and his mind. I should give six months to this preliminary training. The child is probably now ready for learning how to read the alphabet, and when he is able to do so rapidly, he is ready to learn simple drawing and when he has learnt to draw geometrical figures... he will draw not scrawl the figures of the alphabet.[54]

In Gandhian scheme of education, the hand will handle tools before it draws, the eyes will read the pictures of letters and words as they will know other things in life and the ears will catch the names and meanings of things and sentences. As the whole training is natural and responsive, it is quick and easy.[55]

Basic Education

The system of basic education proposed by Gandhi leads to the development of the mind, body and soul whereas the ordinary system of education cares only for the mind.[56] Literacy for him is not the end of education and it is not even the beginning of education. It is only a means to educate the people but literacy is no education. Gandhi wishes that child's education should begin with the teaching of a useful handicraft. This enables the child to produce from the moment the child begins his training. This helps every school to be self-supporting. Under such system of education, the highest development of mind and soul becomes possible. Every handicraft needs to be taught not in a mechanical manner alone but scientifically. The child has to be in a position to know every process of it. The proposal introduced by Gandhi is of revolu-tionary type which saves immense labour. It is economical on the other hand.[57]

Education and Villages

Gandhi thinks that the villages have become a mere

appendage to the cities. They exist to be exploited by the cities. Of the cities make adequate return to the villages for the strength and sustenance they derive from the villages, a healthy and moral relationship will be established between these two. If the city children are to play their part in this great and noble work of social reconstruction, the vocations through which they receive their education ought to be directly related to the requirements of the villages. This will provide a healthy and moral basis of relationship between the city and the village. This helps to eradicate some of the worst evils of the present social insecurity and poisioned relationship between the classes. Gandhian plan of primary education is to impart through the medium of village handicrafts for instance like spinning and carding. This type of education is conceived as the spearhead of a silent social revolution fraught with the most far-reaching consequences. This provides a healthy and moral basis of relationship betweens the city and village. This leads a long way towards eradicating some of the worst evils of present social insecurity and poisoned relationship between eh classes.[58]

The teachers and students working and learning together should derive lessons from the natural and social environments intimately connected with the process of productive work. Thus the catchment area of learning consists of the natural and social environments and the process of productive work. The teachers and students would build up cooperatively as integrated social community sharing in turn all community work, developing self-reliance as a measure of self-sufficiency. All this has to be based on the self-government of the students. Under this the School Assembly would elect a Cabinet of student ministers for planning and carrying out community work inside and outside the school self-assessing, achievements and failures.[59]

Gandhian concept of education aims at the development of all the faculties latent in boys and girls end the all-round growth of their personality not only as individual human beings but also as partakers in building a just; peaceful and progressive society.[60]

Gandhi has put all his reasoning against the common dialogue between learning and working. He wants to have work to vitalize learning and learning to vitalize work. He therefore sometimes refers to basic education as education in and through work.[61] Productive work in basic education is only a means but not an end in itself.

In the earlier educational experiments of Gandhi, he has probably stressed productive work laying stress on intellectual development. These two are kept as separate process. Lateon Gandhi could realize the mistake and has give equal emphasis to both and put them together into one integrated process of learning through work and working for learning.[62]

In the elementary education during the first eight years ought not to be wholly textbook centered and another thing altogether is that books can be given up completely. Books will be certainly necessary. Pinning the minds of boys and girls to textbooks leading to cramming and memorizing need to be avoided. Although memorizing is necessary, it should not be forced through the textbook system Education is more than memorizing and concentrating on specific lessons from the textbooks. But it stands against making the elementary education text book centered. It is not the use of textbooks that is objectionable but the misuse of textbooks. Progressive education has brought about a radical change in the traditional role of teachers. The teacher is not a mere person who just teaches but one who assists children to learn.

Productive work as an instrument of learning is imperative in basic education. If productive work contributes to knowledge under various heads, such work has to be planned, assessed, regulated and executed as educational projects of work. Planning and regulating productive work from very simple beginnings onwards, has to be carefully and scientifically done. Productive work has to be consistent with the age groups of children. In the beginning, production in the form or workship will yield little. Later on the produce of innumerable boys and girls will not be inconsiderable. The produce should belong to the management. This might help in expanding elementary education in a developing country like ours. This idea was changed later on. It was considered proper that what ever the children produced should belong to themselves under the terms and conditions in India, self-sufficiency has come largely to mean giving every child in a basic school – one noon meal a day and two sets of clothes per year. Many children are prevented from coming to school due to lack of these two. In case these could be supplied through the productive work of a basic school that school would be full of children. Some percentage of children would not need these as their parents are well off but majority of the boys and girls would need them. Boys and girls studying in upper classes would produce more and make up for the under production they made in the lower classes. Teacher would work with the children. Whenever parents or relations offer their voluntary help that also would be encouraged.[63]

Productive work has to be conceived more as an instrument of education than for productivity. Productivity in terms, of economic, value is only a necessary corollary but productivity should not be stressed at the cost of intellectual growth. As Gandhi pointed out, the test of success is not simply the self-supporting character. But the whole personality has to be drawn out and developed through productive work in a scientific manner.[64] Every teacher has to learn one major and one subsidiary craft. There are certain broad standards set to evaluate his productive capacity. The teacher has to learn a number of subjects like child an adult psychology, school administration, language teaching and the contents of the syllabus etc. He has to learn specially the method of assisting children to learn through experience and by linking experience with knowledge and understanding. This implies that the teacher has to get a sound working knowledge of the science and art of correlation.[65]

Correlation is the method of linking experience and learning together. This might appear to be over simplication. But experience in this context covers three areas namely the natural environment, the social environment and the processes of productive work. If all these three areas are carefully studied and fully utilized, there is hardly any knowledge, the elementary school boys and girls need to acquire. Learning from experience is more natural, fruitful and simpler than through books.

The teacher has to handle correlation carefully and precisely. He has also to enable learning by children to be an expiating and joyful process by handling correlation also as an artist.

Conditions of the Basic Teacher

Ramachandran says that a Basic teacher has to fulfil the following conditions:

1. Mastery of one major craft and good knowledge of one or two subsiding crafts.
2. Full knowledge of the subject contents of the syllabus under different headings, which means a good deal of brushing up of general knowledge.
3. Practice of community living based on their own self-government and sharing in community work.
4. Appropriate practice teaching not only in a model school attached to the training school but in a few ordinary Basic schools nearby, emphasing the art of training at every stage.
5. Continuous increase of general knowledge through discussions reading and group study.

6. Practice in organizing various types of productive activities and experience in relation to the subject matter contents of the syllabus.
7. Application of the law of love in practice to all situations in the training schools as a prelude to doing the same later in the Basics schools.[66]
8. Basic education does not allow any physical punishment of children under the student self-government, and discipline is evolved from within corrections made as part of self-assessment.[67]

Dr. Saiyedain holds that Gandhi wanted education to be moulded into certain pattern because the good life as he saw could not come into being. Good life or good education is possible only when there is good social order wherein descent men and women could live fruitfully.[68]

Contemplation of non-violence in relation to the problems of India's millions has led Gandhi to arrive at the conclusion that the system of education which is required would have to be such as should be able to pay its way, enabling them to provide themselves, through their own effort which is a means for a healthy descent cultural existence and to train not only their intellect but also their physical and spiritual faculties, with experience Gandhi reveals that what men do with their hands, in order to live, conditions their thinking and behaviour and entire outlook more than what are taught by word or mouth. By correlating the teaching and practice of a socially useful manual craft, the intellectual, physical and spiritual faculties of the child can be fully developed.[69]

> "The basic school of his conception" says Pyarelal, "was thus to be not an idyllic spot far removed from the problems of every-day life facing the child but a laboratory, where the child would be taught to find and test solutions of the problems in individuals and community living facing them and their villages in a

> non-violent and democratic way, so that when they entered life, they would go fully equipped not only with the necessary knowledge but also the spirit of initiative, self-reliance and self-confidence begotten of their experience of learning through doing. And since their knowledge would have grown out of their practice of a truthful non-violent and democratic way of life, it would carry with it the guarantee that it would be rightly used".[70]

Gandhi has much liking for spinning, weaving and the allied processes as the medium for basic education on account of their universality, inter-relation with a prime human need, and little expense. Gandhi said that if the experiment is efficiently conducted the work of the school teachers and children combined as a whole should cover the current expense of the school, i.e., provision for teacher's support and school contingencies, taking the seven year's period covered by basic training as a whole. Self-sufficiency laid down stands as a test of the efficiency of the experiment but not as a condition.

The scope of basic education as envisaged by Gandhi is very wide extended to the children, their parents that should include education for everybody at every stage. The basic school teacher has to consider himself as a universal teacher.

Finally Gandhi says:

Gandhi is regarded as one of the great teachers of human society. His educational ideas and thought were reflected in his writings an speeches with clarity and practicality. In the emerging society ideals and ideas on education are proved to be significant and relevant.

The traditional type of education was mostly literary and theoretical Gandhi felt the system of education to be unsuitable to the needs of the people. There should necessarily be a close contact between the teachers and the taught.

While teaching the craft and other subjects, there is need to lay stress on the principles of cooperative activity, planning accuracy. For Gandhi, craft is only a means of production for the prevailing economic conditions of India but it is also a source of recreation and character building. He attached spiritual significance to the craft centered education.

The craft centered education contributes to the moral and spiritual development. Gandhi's idea of social justice is adequately taken care of in his craft centered education. People will not be subject to exploitation; communal hatred and idleness. Crafts will be productive and self-supporting. By craft and manual work in the scheme of Gandhi's education; Gandhi felt that the child can be improved.

For Gandhi character building is the goal of education. He holds that literacy is neither the beginning nor the end of education. He stated tht literary training by itself adds not an inch to ones moral height and character building is independent of literary training.[71]

> Our education does not provide us with the equality to discriminate between right and wrong and to bridge the gap between our prophecy and practice. Hence thinking at the abstract level keeps us on the ivory tower untouched by the reality of life. Hence the ideals of liberty equality, fraternities etc. are considered desirable on thought level and meant for others rather than our selves. Even if we deviate from these ideals, we are hardly aware of it.[72]

For Gandhi the values of education are not meant for intellectual discussion but to become a method to operate and become a part of human life. Gandhian aim of education is human change and transformation but not merely to acquire knowledge or information.

In the words of Prof. Ramjee Singh:

> "Today ethics, morality compassion and such values

> are accepted in theory but are difficult to implement in practice where as Gandhi thinks that the very implementation of these values in practical life is the very core of education."[73]

There has been progressive deterioration of human values resulting in the erosion of moral life. This is a very dangerous sign. Education is the only way to regulate the conduct of human life. Man cannot become moral under threat, compulsion or coercion. It is only through education, which creates a sense of responsibility and awareness that man could realize the evils that have beset the society and find a way to rid exploitation violence and hatred.

A comprehensive, operationally viable and morally reoriented educational system imbued with values has to be imparted to have lasting effect on the society and achieve good results. On the other hand modernization does not mean to ignore spiritual or moral values.

The education commissions lament over the weakening in the inculcation of moral values in the younger generation. So there is need to make education value oriented to make it more relevant and useful. Kothari Commission Report laments over the absence offer not making provision of social, moral and spiritual values in the field of education. The report holds that "in the life of the majority of Indians, religion is motivating force and is intimately bound up with the formation of character and inculcation of ethical values'[74]

It is culture of heart and the development of character that becomes the upper most in the mind of Gandhi Knowledge becomes valueless in the absence of character. The true aim of education is to prepare a man for a profession and also to make him perform functions other than the production and transmission of wealth for his self-preservation.

Education is the most powerful instrument of social transformation. Gandhi had revolutionary ideas about educational goals. Apart from intellectual pursuit for knowledge other aspects such as character building etc. assume importance. Individual development has to go hand in hand with society. So individualistic values of education are not correct. In order to make education relevant, it must necessarily cultivate the value of peace and Peace. Research is need for the preservation of present civilization.[75]

Mahatma Gandhi was classed among those who thoroughly studied state and conditions prevailing in the society. He made his educational philosophy more relevant to the needs of the people. Gandhi made a through study of the socio-economic situation of India in compassion to the world situation. He formulated the educational polices so as to suit the requirements of India.

For Gandhi truth and Ahimsa are the means for religion. He held that truth is inclusive of ahimsa an indispensable means for the discovery of truth. According to him that any thing that promotes the practice of these virtues is a means for imparting religions education and the best way for the teachers is to practice these virtues.

With regard to instruction in the universal essentials of religion he held that a curriculum of religious instruction should include a study of the tenets of faith other than their own He stated that for this purpose the students should be in such a manner so as to cultivate the habit of understanding and appreciating the doctrines of different great religions of the world in a spirit of reverence and broad minded tolerance Gandhi says that:

> "The study of other religions besides one's own will give one a grasp of the rock-bottom unity of all religions and afford a glimpse also of that universal and absolute truth which lies beyond the dust of creeds and faiths."[76]

REFERENCES

1. George. H. Sabine, *A Study of Political Theory,* p. 69.
2. J.S. Mathur, *Facets of Gandhian Thought,* p. 95.
3. *Selections from Bose,* p. 251.
4. *Harijan,* 10.3.1946, p, 38.
5. *Ibid.,* 19.1.1947, p. 494.
6. *Selections from Bose,* p. 256.
7. *Ibid.,* p. 258
8. *Harijan,* 7.11.1936. p. 309.
9. *Ibid.,* 8.3.1935. p. 28.
10. M.K. Gandhi, *The Story of My Experiments with Truth,* p. 251.
11. *Selections from Bose,* pp. 261-64.
12. *Ibid,* pp. 263-66
13. Gisbert Pascuel, *Fundamentals of Sociology,* Orient Longmans, Bombay, p. 210.
14. *Harijan,* 31-7-1937, P. 197.
15. Prof. V. Gopalakrishnaih, *New Facets of Eastern and Western Philosophy of Education,* pp. 1-2.
16. Carter V. Good, *Dictionary of Education,* McGraw Hill Book Company, New York, 1979, p. 420.
17. *The Encyclopedia of Education. Preface,* p. viii.
18. Lee C. Deighgton (ed), *Encyclopedia of Philosophy of Education,* p. 101, The Macmillan Company, USA., 1971.
19. Joe Park (ed), *Selected Readings in the Philosophy of Education,* pp. 3-4.
20. John Dewey, *Democracy and Education,* p. 324.
21. *Ibid.,* p. 331
22. Joe Park (ed), *Selected Readings in the Philosophy of Education,* p. 5.
23. Theodore Bramald, *Education as Power,* p. 32. (New York, Bene hart and Winston Inc. 1965).
24. *Ibid.,* p. 224
25. Joe Park, *Selected Readings in the Philosophy of Education,* p. 128.
26. John Dewey, *Democracy and Education,* p. 110.
27. Mudaliar Commission, *Secondary Education Commission Report,* (1952-53), p. 24.

28. M.K. Gandhi, *True Education*, p. 13.
29. *Ibid.*, P. 22.
30. *Ibid.*, PP. 40-41.
31. *Ibid.*, P. 39.
32. *Young India*, 13-10-1927, p. 342.
33. M. K. Ganmdhi, *True Education*, p. 127.
34. *Young India*, 6-12-1928. p. 406.
35. *Harijan*, 23-3-1947. p. 76.
36. *Ibid.*, P. 76.
37. M.K. Gandhi, *Towards New Education*, p. 20.
38. Suresh Chandra Ghosh, *The History of Education in Modern India, 1757-1998*, pp. 166-167.
39. Dr. C.P.S. Chauhan, *Modern Indian Education: Policies Progress and Problems*. p. 37.
40. M.K. Gandhi, *Basic Education*, p. 52.
41. Dr. CPS. Chauhan, *op.cit.*, p. 36.
42. *Ibid.*, P. 37.
43. *Harijan*, 9-11-1947, p. 401.
44. *Selections from Bose*, pp. 256-57.
45. *Harijan*, 8-9-1946, p. 306.
46. Ramachandran, (ed). *Quest for Gandhi*, p. 332.
47. *Ibid.*, p. 332.
48. Pyarelal, *Mahatma Gandhi, The Last Phase*, Vol. I, Book I, P. 54.
49. G. Ramachandran, *Quest for Gandhi*, P. 334.
50. *Harijan*, 10-11-1946, p. 394.
51. *Ibid.*, 11-9-1937, p. 256.
52. *Ibid.*, 21-12-1947, p. 480.
53. *Ibid.*, 9-11-1947, p. 145.
54. *Ibid.*, 5-6-1937, p. 130.
55. *Ibid.*, 28-8-1937, p. 225.
56. *Selections from Bose*, pp. 256-57.
57. *Harijan*, 8.9.1946. p. 306.
58. *Harijan*, 9-10-1937, p. 293.
59. G. Ramachandran (Ed), *Quest for Gandhi*, p. 333.
60. *Ibid.*, p. 334.

61. *Ibid.*, p. 334.
62. *Ibid.*, p. 336.
63. *Ibid.*, p. 337.
64. *Ibid.*, p. 337.
65. *Ibid.*, pp. 339-40.
66. *Ibid.*, pp. 339-40.
67. *Ibid.*, p. 340.
68. J. S. Mathur (ed), *Facets of Gandhian Thought*, p. 94.
69. Pyarelal, *Mahatma Gandhi*, Vol. I, Book One, *The Last Phase*, p. 55.
70. *Ibid.*
71. M.K. Gandhi, *Young India*, 1.6.1921. p. 170
72. Ramjee Singh, *Gandhi and the Modern World*, p. 224.
73. *Ibid*, p. 224.
74. *Report of the Education Commission*, p. 358.
75. Ramjee singh, *Gandhi and the Modern World*, p. 232.
76. *Young India*, 10-12-28, p. 406.

10

Trusteeship

Mahatma Gandhi held that to achieve non-violent independence economic equality is the master key. Economic equality can be established only if the eternal conflict between capital and labour is abolished which means the levelling down of the few rich in whose hands the bulk of nations wealth is concentrated on the one hand, and. the levelling up of the semi-starved naked millions on the other. He pointed out theft a non-violent system of government is clearly an impossibility so long as the wide gulf between the rich and the hungry millions persists. He said that a violent and bloody revolution would, be one day a certainty unless there would be a voluntary abdication of riches and the power that riches give and share them for the common good.[1]

Gandhi obtained the idea of trusteeship when he was a student of legal studies in England. He found this idea also in the *Gita*. He tried to apply this idea as solu-tion to the existing economic inequalities. He felt that inequalities could not be removed out of society unless the rich and the poor were morally awakened to the consciousness of their own duties, defects and weaknesses. An appeal to reason love could bring about such awareness and the efforts for self-purification.[2]

Capital and Labour

In the opinion of Gandhi labour was far superior to capital. In the absence of labour, gold, silver and copper were a useless burden for it was labour which extracted precious ore from the bowels of the earth.[3] D.M. Datta held that Gandhi thus came quite close to Marxs labour theory of value. He like Marxs thought that the combination of labour against capital could subvert capitalism. Gandhi would not incite labour against capital nor would encourage the overthrow of capitalists by-force. The use of force in this process would be based on class hatred which undermines the moral principle of *ahimsa.* No society could thrive on hatred and violence in any form. As it is immoral for the capitalists to steal the legitimate fruits of the workers labour, it is also immoral for labourers to the industries and tyrannize the capitalists by unwanted demands.[4]

Gandhi pointed out:

> By the non-violent method we seek not to destroy the capitalist, we seek to destroy capitalism. We invite the capitalists to regard himself as a trustee for those on whom he depends for the making, the retention and the increase of his capital. Nor need the worker wait for his conversion. If capital is power, so is work. Either power can be used destructively or creatively. Either is dependent on the Other. Immediately the worker realizes his strength, he is in a position to become co-sharer with the capitalist instead of remaining his slave.[5]

Gandhi wanted a marriage between capital and labour. His ideal was that capital and labour should supplement and help each other. Key wanted theft they should be a great family living in unity and harmony. Capital has not only to look to the material welfare of the laboures, but also their moral welfare also. Capitalists have to be trustees for the welfare of the labouring classes under them.[2] Gandhi was not against capital but against capitalism.

Gandhi believed that it would be possible to appeal to the basic human principles of reason and love to persuade capitalists to realize that the capital in their hands represented the fruit of the labour of the people and it should be treated as such. A capitalist or a landlord who has surplus wealth, should as the trustee of people's wealth. He should spend it for the welfare of the people. He should have the realization about the evils and dangers of accumulation of wealth. He should also see that it is in his own larger interest to use his wealth for the people, rather than for his personal comforts. Then capitalists would exist as trustees. On that happy day, there would be no difference between capital and labour. The labour would have ample food, good and sanitary dwellings, all the necessary education and proper medical assistance then.[7]

Welfare of the Community

Gandhi invited those people who consider themselves as owners today to act as trustees. The ownership they had is not in their own right, but owners in the right of those whom they have exploited.[8] If some came by a fair amount of wealth either by a way of legacy, or by means of trade and industry, he must realize the fact that all wealth does not belong to him. "What belongs to him is the right to have an honorable livelihood, which is net better than that enjoyed by millions of others. The rest of his wealth belongs to the community which must be used for the welfare of the community. Gandhi held that he enunciated the theory of, ownership and trustee-ship when the socialist theory was placed, before the country in respect of the possessions held by seminars and ruling chiefs. Gandhi wanted that they should out-grow their greed and sense of passion, and to come down inspire of their wealth to the level of those who earn their bread by labour.

There is need for the labourer to realize that the wealthy man is less owner of his wealth than the labourer is owner of his own, viz. the power to work.[9]

Not Makeshift

The theory of trusteeship advocated by Gandhi is no makeshift and there is no camouflage. Gandhi was confident that this theory would survive all other theories. He held that it has the sanction of philosophy and religion behind it. If the possessers of wealth have not acted upto the theory it does not prove its falsity; but it proves the weakness of the wealthy. No other theory is compatible with non-violence. Through non-violence and non-cooperation, the wrong-doer is made to see the error he finds himself completely isolated.[10]

Acquisition of Wealth

Gandhi asked such of those who possesses money to behave like trustees, holding their riches on behalf of the poor. It may be said that trusteeship is a legal fiction. But if the people meditate over it constantly and act up to it, their life on earth would be governed by love and it be better than the present. He held that absolute trusteeship is an abstraction like Euclids definition of a point. It is equally unattainable. If people strive for it, they will be able to go further in realizing the state of equality on earth than by any other method.[11]

He was of the opinion that it would, be possible to acquire riches without consciously doing wrong. But he accepted the proposition that it is better not to desire wealth than to acquire it and become its trustee. He could only advise those who are already wealthy to use their wealth for service. Gandhi accepted it as truth that generally the rich spend, more on themselves than they need which can be avoided. The well-to-do should educate and bring up the children so that they may learn to be independent, but this is not done. Those who consider it a duty to adopt poverty and believe in the desire of economic equality may not be jealous of the rich. They should exhibit real happiness in their poverty which others may emulate. He said that a trustee has no heir but the public. In .the state built on the basis of non-violence, the Commission of trustees will be regulated.[12]

The Choice to be Made

Gandhi said that the present owners of wealth have to make their choice between class war and voluntarily converting themselves as trustees of their wealth. They will be allowed to retain the stewardship of their possessions and to use their talent to increase the wealth, not for their own sake but for the sake of the nation without exploitation. The state will regulate the rate of commission which they get. It would commensurate with the service rendered and its value to society. Their children would inherit the stewardship if they are proved to be fit for it.

When the people understand the implication of trusteeship and the atmosphere is ripe for it, they themselves would begin to introduce such statues beginning with gram panchayats. It has to come from below to be successful. If it comes from above, it is liable to be a deed weight.[13]

Non-violent Economy

Gandhi held that economies "which hurt the moral well-being of an individual or a nation are immoral and there-fore sinful. Thus the economics that permit one country to prey upon another are immoral."[14] That type of economics which ignores or disregards moral values is untrue. He considered the extension of the law of non-violence in the domain of economics is nothing less than the introduction of moral values as a factor to be considered in regulating international commerce.[15]

Ideal Economy

According to Gandhi the economic constitution of India and for the matter of that the world should be such that no one under it should suffer for want of food and clothing. This implies that everybody should be able to get sufficient work to enable himself to make the book ends meet. This ideal can be universally realized only if the means of production of elementary necessaries of life remain in the control of the masses. These should be freely available to all as Gods air and water. But they should not be made a vehicle of traffic for the exploitation of others. This would be unjust. The neglect of this simple principle is felt to be the cause of destitution.[16] True economics does not stand. Against the highest ethical standard. An economics that enables the strong to assess wealth at the expense of the weak is a false and dismal science. True economics stands for social justice. It promotes the good of all equally including the weakest. It is indispensable for decent life.[17]

Minimum Violence

No activity and no industry are possible without a certain amount of violence. Even the very process of living involves a certain amount of violence. Gandhi said that we have to minimize the violence to the greatest extent possible. Since all activity in life involves some measure of violence, we have to minimize the violence involved in it. This is not possible without a strong belief in non-violence. A non-violent occupation is fundamentally free from violence which involves no exploitation or envy of others.[18]

Rural Economics

The village economics which are organized on the basis of non-violent occupations earned, their living. Their labour contributed to the good of the community. Body labour was at the care of these occupations and industries. There was no large-scale machinery. When man is content to own only so much land as he can till with his own labour he cannot exploit others. Handi-crafts exclude exploitation and slavery. Large-scale machinery concentrates wealth in the hands of one man. He holds of it over the rest who slave for him. He may be trying to create ideal conditions for his workmen. It is nothing but exploitation which is a form of violence. When the society is not based on exploitation but on justice/truth and non-violence are not virtues confined to individuals but are practiced by communities.[19]

Economic Equality

Gandhi held that his idea of society is that while all are born equal all have the right to have equal opportunity. All have not the same capacity. It is in the nature of things impossible. For instance, all can not have the same height, or colour, or degree of intelligence. Therefore, in the nature of things some will have ability to earn more and others less. People with talents will have more ability to earn and they will utilize their talents for this purpose. If they utilize their talents with kindness, they will be performing the work of the state. Such people exist as trustees without any other terms. Gandhi was not against a man of intellect who earns more and he did not cramp his talent. But he wanted that the bulk of his greater earnings must be used for the good of the State which is same as the income of all earning sons of the father goes to the common family fund. They would have their earnings only as trustees.[20]

Removal of Disparity

In Gandhi's conception, economic equality does not mean that everyone will literally have the same amount. It simply means that everybody should have enough for his or her needs. The real meaning of economic equality is "To each according to his need" is the definition of Marx. If a simple man demands as much es a man with wife and four children/ that is a violation of economic equality.

Gandhi observed that the contrast between the rich and the poor today is a painful sight. The poor villagers are exploited by the city dwellers. They produce food but they go hungry. They produce milk but their children go without milk. This is disgraceful. He wanted that everyone must have a balanced diet, a decent house to live in, facilities for the education of children and adequate medical relief and under his plan the state would carryout the will of the people. But the state is not to dictate or force them to do its will. Gandhi aimed at bringing about economic equality through non-violence by converting the people to his point of view by harnessing the forces of love as against hatred.[21]

Gandhi held that accumulation of capital by private persons is not possible except through violent means. But accumulation of wealth by state is desirable and possible in a non-violent society.[22] At present there is gross economic inequality. The basis of socialism is economic equality.[23]

Doctrine of Equal Distribuion

The national power can be organized by adopting the best methods of production alone but by the best methods of production and distribution.[24] The ideal of Gandhi is equal distribution but he could see that it could not be realized. So he worked out for equitable distribution.[25]

New Social Order

To bring about an ideal of economic equality, the entire social order has to got to be reconstructed. As the progress towards that goal is made, contentment and happiness could be found. It is possible for an individual to adopt the way of life without wanting for others. But the individual has to observe a certain rules of conduct as that others may follow.[26]

Equal Distribution through Non-violence

Equal distribution can be brought about through non-violence. It involves some chance in personal life to be brought about on the part of the person who stands for this ideal. He has to reduce his wants to the minimum bearing in mind poverty of the country. His earnings would be free of dishonesty. He would lead a new mode of life with self-restraint exercised in every sphere of life. When this ideal is realized in his own life, then only it would be possible for him to preach about the ideal among his associates and neighbours. At the root of this doctrine must be the doctrine of the trusteeship of the wealthy for the superfluous wealth possessed by them. According to the doctrine they must not possess even a rupee more than their neighbours.

This cannot be achieved by resorting to violence as violent action .cannot benefit the society for it would lose the gifts of the society who knows how to accumulate wealth. Non-violence is evidently superior. The rich man will be left in possession of his riches and would what he reasonably needs for his personal needs. He will act as a trustee for the remainder to be used for the society.[27]

Change of Heart

As soon as man thinks of the welfare of the society, he earns for its sake, and spends for its sake. Thereby purity enters into his earnings. If the minds of men are turned towards this way of life, peaceful revolution would come about in society without any bitterness.[28]

Practical Formula of Trusteeship

The following formula of trusteeship is simple and practical. This was drawn up by Kishorlal Mashruwala and Narahari Parikh. This was approved by Gandhi with a few-changes.

1. "Trusteeship provides a means of transforming the present capitalist order of society into an egalitarian one. It gives no quarter to capitalism, but gives the

present owning class a chance of reforming itself. It is based on the faith that human nature is never beyond redemption.

2. It does not recognize any right of private ownership of property except so far as it may be permitted by society for its own welfare.

3. It does not exclude legislative regulation of the ownership and use of wealth.

4. Thus under state regulated trusteeship, an individual will not be free to hold or use his wealth for selfish satisfaction or in disregard of the interests of society.[29]

5. Just as it is proposed to fix a decent minimum living wage, even so a limit should be fixed for the maximum income that would be allowed and to any person in society. The difference between such minimum and maximum incomes should be reasonable and equitable and variable from time to time so much so that the tendency would be towards obliteration of the difference.

6. Under the Gandhi an economic 'order the character of production will be determined by social necessity and not by personal whim or greed.[30]

REFERENCES

1. M.K. Gandhi, *Constructive Programme: Its Meaning and Phage*, pp. 20-21.
2. D.M. Datta,*The Philosophy of Mahatma Gandhi*, pp. 109-10.
3. *Ibid.*, pp. 109-10
4. M.K. Bose, *Selections From Gandhi*, pp.2 3 4-35.
5. D.M. Datta, *The Philosophy of Mahatma Gandhi*, p. 108,
6. *Young India*, 26.3.1931, p. 49.
7. *Ibid.*, 20.8.1925, p. 285.
8. D.M. Datta, *The Philosophy of Mahatma Gandhi*, p.109.

9. *Young India*, 26..11.1931, p.369.
10. *Harijan*, 3.6.1939, p. 145.
11. *Ibid.*, 16.11.1939, p. 376.
12. *Modern Review*, October 1935, p. 412.
13. *Harijan*, 12.4.1942, p. 116.
14. *Ibid.*, 31.3.1946, pp. 63-64.
15. *Young India*, 13.10.1921, p. 325.
16. *Ibid.*, 27.10.1921, p. 344.
17. *Young India*, 15.11.1928, p. 381.
18. *Harijan*, 9.10.1937, p. 292.
19. *Ibid.*, 1.9.19 40, p. 271,
20. *Ibid.*, 1.9.19 40, p. 27 2.
21. *Young India*, 26.11.1931. p. 368.
22. *Ibid.*, 31.3.1946, p. 63.
23. *Harijan*. 16.2.19 47, p. 25.
24. *Ibid.*, 1.6.1947, p. 172.
25. *Young India*, 8.7.1920, p. 5.
26. *Ibid.*, 17.3.1927, p. 36.
27. *Harijan*, 25.8.1940, p. 260
28. *Harijan*, 25.8.1940, p. 261.
29. *Ibid.*, 25.8.1940, p. 260.
30. *Ibid.*, 25.10.1952, p. 301.

11

Democracy

Democracy literally means power of the people. Modern democracy is meant to protect the freedom of the individual. Democracy is based on the doctrine of self-rule.

In the words of Gandhi democracy in essence must mean "the art and science of mobilizing the entire physical, economic and spiritual resources of all the various sections of the people in the service cf the common good of all".[1] In his conception democracy or serving as he calls it is not restricted to a select few but it is the self-rule by many. True democracy will emerge not by the acquisition of authority by a few at the cost of the rest. All the people have to be given equal opportunity for self-development to enable them to participate in the activities of democracy freely. Swaraj of a people means the sum total of the *Swaraj* of a people means the total of the Swaraj of individuals. The spirit of democracy is not a mechanical thing to be adjusted by abolition of forms. It requires the change of heart, and the inculcation of the spirit of brotherhood.

Discipline

Gandhi lays more stress on the need for the people to be disciplined in the activities of their lives. Without observing discipline they cannot achieve any thing. In his opinion, a born democrat is a born discipline. Democracy comes naturally from the people by their observance of all laws grounded in morality. The highest form of freedom carries with it the greatest measure of discipline, and humanity. Freedom that comes from discipline and humility cannot be denied. Unburied license is a sign of vulgarity injurious alike to self- and one's neighbours. When democracy is disciplined and enlightened, it is the finest thing in the world. A democracy which is prejudiced ignorant and superstitious, will lead itself in chaos. It may be self destructive.

Responsibility of the Individual

According to Gandhi, the real democracy works out for the full freedom and growth of the individual. He holds that the first. Step to *Swaraj* (Democracy) lies with the individual, he says that it is the responsibility of every man and woman to think for himself or herself in true democracy. This revolution like charity can be brought about, if it begins at home.

In democracy individual will is governed and limited by the social will which is the state. The state is governed by and for democracy. Every individual has to take into consideration the interest and will of the society. If every individual takes the law into his own hands, there is no state. It becomes anarchy and lawless. That way results in destruction of liberty. Therefore it is the responsibility of the individuals to create the conditions of peace end order to facilitate the state to secure justice.

The Test of Democracy

The truest test of democracy lies in the ability of anyone to act as he likes. So long as one does not injure the life or property of any one else, he is successful in the test. It is not possible to control public morals by the acts of violence. A demarcate is one who completely identifies with the poorest of mankind with an intense longing to live no better than them. When the democrat has corresponding conscious effort to approach that level to the best of his ability can entitle him to make the test.

Democracy comes naturally to him who is habituated normally to yield willing obedience to all laws; human or divine. A democrat must first of all qualify himself by satisfying this acid list of democracy if he is ambitions to serve democracy. A democrat must be utterly selfless. He must think and dream not in terms of self or party but only of democracy. Gandhi does not went anybody to give up his connections or to suppress himself. He believes that a healthy and honest difference of opinion will not injure the cause. But opportunism, patched-up compromises certainly will injure the cause. The opinions must be genuine but should not be of a party. Democracy can exist only in trust. The democracy lies in the labour.

Representation in Democracy

Gandhi holds that it is an utter delusion to believe that a large number of delegates is in any way a help to the better conduct of business or that it safe guards the principle of democracy. Fifteen hundred delegates, zealous of the interests of the people broad minded and truthful, would anybody be a fetter safeguard for democracy than six thousand irresponsible men chosen any how. To safeguard democracy, the people must have a keen sense of independence, self-respect and their oneness. The people should insist on choosing only such persons as are good and true as their representatives.

True democracy is not inconsistent with a few persons representing the spirit, the hope end the aspirations of those whom they claim to represent. Gandhi holds that democracy cannot be evolved by forcible methods. The spirit of democracy cannot be imposed from without but it has to come from within.

The very essence or democracy is that every person represents all the varied interests which compose the nation. It is true that it does not exclude and should not exclude special representation of special interests. Such representation is not its test but a sign of imperfection. Surely timidity has no place in democracy where people in general believe to want a particular thing. Their representatives have but to give shape to their demand and make feasible.

The Voice of People

The voice of people may be said to be voice of God and the voice of panchayat. When the people themselves are turned out to be exploiters, there cannot be the voice of God. If the voice of the people is the voice of God, they will be above party.

It is necessary for the people to keep themselves in constant touch with those whom they put in power. There is need for the people in a democracy to draw the attention of the government to mistakes if any. They could remove the government of they wish to. In democracy peoples will must rule.

Majority and Minority in Democracy

Gandhi realized that in popular government, majority view hest to be basis of particular action. So he says that the rule of majority has a narrow application for one should invariably yield to the majority in the matters of detail (Particular items). He considers this as mere slavery to be amenable to the majority no matter what its decisions are. Gandhi says that democracy is not a state in which people oct like sheep. Under democracy individual liberty of opinion and action is zealously guarded. So Gandhi believes that minority has a perfect right to act differently from the majority. So he wants government not based on concern even of a minority but on its conversion. In the democracy, as Gandhi visualizes the minority would not be coerced but only persuaded, respected and converted. In order to get the just things done, the majority has to follow the methods of pursuance and even self suffering, lest the tyranny of the majority should have place in democracy.

Gandhi holds that in the matters of conscience the law of majority has no place. In order to achieve the amicable and smooth relations between the majority and minority, Gandhi aims at the attitude of tolerance to be developed. Gandhi prescribes tolerance to the majority so that majority rule may prevail when it is morally binding and the opinions of minority may be respected. He says in a press conference that the rule of majority does not mean that it should suppress the opinion of even an individual if it is sound. The opinion of an individual should have greeter weight than the opinion of many if the opinion is sound in merits. That is the view of real democracy of Gandhi. One should not become slaves to the resolutions of majorities. In a good democracy, the majority should be democratic enough to see with sympathy that the minority's interests do not suffer. On the other hand, the minority should be bold enough to stand up for their moral and legitimate aspirations and should fight for them in the non-violent ways. But Gandhi believes that the individuals and minorities are out to be ignored and neglected in huge representa-tive septum's of government. Therefore, he strongly favours a federation of decentralized units of ideal village republic.

Intolerance

If one wants to cultivate a true spirit of democracy he should not afford to be intolerant. He observes that no school of thought can claim a monopoly of right judgment. People have to try to understand the opponent's view point. If they cannot accept it, let it be respected as they expect him to respect theirs. It is one of the indispensable tests of a healthy public life and fitness for *Swaraj* (self-rule). Without charity, and tolerance the differences cannot be settled amicably. Therefore people must always submit the arbitration of a third party. Intolerance, discourtesy and harshness are taboos (banned on ground of morality). They are surely contrary to the spirit of democracy.

Evolution of democracy is not possible if the people are not prepared to her the other side. People refuse to hear to their opponents and make fun of them if they listen. If intolerance becomes a habit, truth will be missed. There is need for the people to act fearlessly. They must always keep an open mind and be ever ready to find that what they believed to be true is after all untruth. This openness of mind, strengthens the truth.

Public Opinion

Public opinion alone can keep a society pure and healthy. A popular state can never act in advance of public opinion. If it goes against it, it will be destroyed. Healthy, well-informed and balanced criticism is the zone of public life. A public opinion is the only force at the disposal of democracy. But it becomes intolerable when it becomes violent and aggressive. Legislation in advance of public opinion is often worse than useless. Non-cooperation is the quickest method of creating public. opinion.

Monocracy

Gandhi emphasizes the need to train the masses of men who have a heart of gold. Who feel for the country and who want to be taught and led. With the help of a few intelligent and sincere local workers the whole nation can be organized, to act intelligently. Democracy can be evolved by monocracy. A democratic organization has to do the right at all cost. But he who ponders to the weakness of a person degrades both himself and the people. He leads them not to democratic but to mob rule.

Militarism

Dependence on the military and the police is incompatible with democracy. Military help would degrade the democratic value. Gandhi holes that democracy and the military spirit are contradictory in terms. A democrat relies upon the force not of the arms of his state but on the moral force. The spirit of democracy cannot be established in the midst of militarism.

Democracy and Non-violence

True democracy can never be based, on violence and force. In order to promote the full and free growth of the individual, democratic society must be based on fellow feeling, reasonable understanding, mutual trust and co-operation. It is on such principles that humanity has so far progressed. It is on them again that mankind can progress still further. The main principle of human love has always inspired man to seek the good of the self in the good of all. To the extent that this principle has been followed, there has been peace among men and men, groups and groups, nations and nations. The principle of love or non-violence should be the basis of every human organization from the smallest unit called the family to the largest organization, the international human family. If any of these component units be immoral i.e., based on violence, hatred, greed and the like, the character of the larger whole will be spoiled by strife, vary and ruin. The peace of happiness of mankind will necessarily be endangered. Democracy can grow only by the voluntary efforts of the individual.

If the States are to become truly democratic, they must become courageously non-violent. If they are nominal, they have to become totalitarian. Gandhi holds that it's blasphemy is a blasphemy to say that non-violence can only be practised by individuals and never by nations which are composed of individuals.

The true democrat is he who with purely non-violent means defends his liberty and his country's and ultimately of the whole of mankind. Gandhi says that true democracy can never come through untruthful and violent means for the simple reason that the natural corollary to their use would be to reinvent all opposition through the suppression or extermination of the antagonists. This does not make for individual freedom. Individual freedom which is of much importance in democracy can have the fullest play only under a régime of undulated *ahimsa* (non-violence).

In the nation of Gandhi democracy is that under which the weakest should have the same opportunity as the strongest. This can be possible only through non-violence. When the democracy is sustained by violence, there is no possibility for the protection of the weak.

Gandhi believes that the true democracy can only be an outcome of non-violence. No perfect democracy is possible without perfect non-violence at the back of it. He holds that non-violence of the weak is the decrial of the basic principle of democracy. Which would never take the people to the good of freedom. The non-violence of the weak would use it is expediency and resorts to violence when the situation demands. Gandhi holes that democracy cannot be evolved by forcible methods. Non-violence plays a dominant role in establishing a true democracy.

Decentralization

Gandhi aims at decentralization of many things if the nature is to evolve along non-violent lines. It is because centralization cannot be sustained and defended without adequate force. Gandhi holds that centralization as a system is inconsistent with non-violent structure of society.

In the centralized type of government there is no scope for the individual initiative and people's participation in the affairs of the state. The power is vested in the hands of a few selected persons in the centralized type of government. He observes that an increase in power of the State with greatest fear because it destroys the individua-lity of individual which has at the root of all progress although it does good apparently by minimizing exploitation. Human participation is possible only in a decentralized type of Government.

In Gandhism decentralized democracy, the dimensional setting of power is geographic. It starts necessarily from the village as a unit based on the self-rule with the individual participation. His idea of decentralization is broad based, thus keeping the village as a unit at the base and the centre at the apex to enable the democratic government to encounter any boomers. Gandhi believes in reconstruction of villages alone to be the effective basis for the emancipation of the centres of national energy for the strength of the political system consists not in the magnification of the state but in the reorganization of the villages through the practice of constructor programme. He aims at the evolving of a decentralized structure of power based on the effective reconstruction of self-reliant and self-sufficient villages. The village organization is to be based on the constructor, social and economic efforts of individual participation and the repudiation of self-interest. Decentralized and autonomous village communities in natural healthy surroundings would help individuals live simpler lives, develop more of social sense, cooperative works intimate neighboring love, and the virtues that follow there from.

Gandhi aims at *swaraj* (self rule) by which he means government by the consent of the people as ascertained by the large number of the adult population, male and female native born or formicated. Ken says that the people should not act like sheep but they should take an active part in determining their own forms of government in accordance with the genius of the people. Self-rule should be sovereignty of the people based on pure moral authority. The participation of people becomes possible only when the government is of decentralized type. His notion of *purna swaraj* (complete self-rule) is not isolated independence but healthy and dignified interdependence.

REFERENCE

1. *Harijan*. 27.5.1939. p. 143.

12

Disarmament and World Peace

Among the contemporary world issues, the problem of peace is vital and significant drawing the attention of all great intellectuals and statesmen. Peace signifies the end of hostilities between those who have been at war or in a state of enmity. It is a freedom from war or civil disorder. It is a state of quietness, blissfulness, tranquility and friendliness.

In a maxim of *Arthasastra*, Kautilya has given much importance to peace with utmost concern. He states "peace is that which allows the enjoyment of results achieved without disturbance."[1] He terms peace and activity as the source of security and welfare.[2] Peace can only be established by social justice but not by exploitation. The lasting peace is attainable by observing the basic moral conditions such as equitable distribution of power, knowledge and income and also by defending human rights.

Gandhi has faith in humanity. He is of the opinion that man is not beyond redemption from his delinquencies. He holds that not to believe in the possibility of permanent peace is to disbelieve in the Godliness of human nature. Methods for the establishment of peace have failed because of the lack of sincerity on the part of those who have striven but they did not realize this.

Peace is unattained due to the partial performance of conditions even as chemical combination is impossible without complete fulfilment of the conditions of attainment thereof, if the recognized leaders of mankind who have control over the engines of destruction are wholly to renounce their use with full knowledge of its implications, permanent peace can be established. This is clearly impossible without the great powers of the earth renouncing their imperialistic design.[3] Peace cannot be established through mere conferences. Peace is being broken even while conferences are being held.[4]

Peace comes only when the Great Powers courageously disarm themselves. Gandhi emphasizes the need to force the Great Powers to disarm themselves as the recent events occurred in the world caused great misery to the humanity.[5] To preserve the fine values of civilization and to enable to live in peace and mutual trust, man must set on a high road to the eventual elimination of military as an institution.[6]

The problem of war and peace is found to be a fundamental and a complex problem of historical development, confronting the humanity. It has become very difficult even for the big powers to prevent the outbreak of a global nuclear war.[7] The destinies and. the lives of the human race depend on the problem of peace and war. The development of new technology has transformed the entire globe into a potential theatre of military operations. If this is allowed a new world war would bring unprecedented disasters.[8]

Doctrine of Deterrence

The doctrine of deterrence is known for several ages but the present doctrine in force is distinguished from the earlier practice. Within the short period, the two sides are capable of reducing the vast areas of the globe to radioactive cinders exterminating method of population without sending a single armed, soldier beyond the boarders of each side. Unlike in the past there will be only a few survivors remaining to regret the folly of having violated the bonds of deterrence. While the earlier practice of deterrence is based on an expectation of survival and infliction of unacceptable damage on the side that violated the *status quo*, the doctrine of nuclear deterrence is entirely based on a threat of mutual suicide.[9]

If we observe the operation of the doctrine of deterrence which responds on the conditional basis we find it perpetuating animosity, hatred, mutual terror and also it results in mistrust. It stands as a barrier in promoting international understanding and cooperation.

The late Prime Minister Smt. Indira Gandhi emphasized the need for the establishment of peace and all the efforts are to be directed towards the goal. She says to the whole world that the doctrine of deterrence has gained a certain amount of academic credibility but it gives rise to a growing sense of insecurity.

> "Our thoughts" says Smt. Indira Gandhi, "turn to the deeper pauses underlying the present uncertainties and fears. The doctrine of deterrence and balance of mutual terror appear to have gained a certain amount of even academic kb credibility. Yet the accumulated evidence of human history leads to the conclusion that armaments and the building up of atomic arsenals are giving rise to a growing sense of insecurity."[10]

Much of our national prosperity and the bulk of scientific endeavour and technological resources are diverted to upgrade the armaments as a result of the doctrine of deterrence. While referring to do the doctrine of deterrence our late Prime Minister of India Shri Rajiv Gandhi pointed out:

> "In consequence of doctrine of deterrence, inter-national relations have been gravely militarized. Astronomical

> sums are being invested in ways of dealing death. Ever new means of destruction continue to be invented. The best of our scientific talent and the bulk of our technological resources are devoted to maintaining and upgrading this awesome ability to obliterate ourselves. The culture of armaments and threats and violence have become pervasive.[11]

Atomic Weapons and Its Destructive Effects

The radioactivity emanates from the nuclear tests and it represents a greater danger for all parts of the world. The bad effects may be made to be felt not only in the first or second generation but do the following generations. Centuries to come would witness the birth of an ever-increasing number of children with mental defects and physical deformities. The land of peoples would be uninhabitant in the atomic war. For this reason the scientists demand for an international agreement to put an end to the nuclear tests.[12]

The country which uses atomic weapons to defend freedom would be subject to a similar fate. Instead, of freedom, he would experience destruction. In an atomic war there would neither be conqueror nor conquered. Both sides experience the same fate during such bombardment.[13] An atomic war is the most senseless, lunatic, inhuman and most dangerous and it should be prevented at any cost.

Non-violence and Peace

Violence and war are found to be mere futile, as violence evokes counter violence and resentment. Wars escalate, brutalize arid make the people more callous. On the other hand, wars breed evils such as hatred and enmity. So we don't find any other alternative except non-violence to be relied on to establish peace. Non-violence is the way of life devoid of all extremes of passions like anger, enmity, pleasure and pain. Non-violence has been most vigorously practised by Jainism.

Gandhi is the pioneer in applying non-violence for the solution of the day to day problems of which the humanity is confronted with. The follower of non-violence treats his fellow being equal and makes a rational appeal to the opponent by even self-suffering and arouses the moral conscience of the opponent. The non-violent resister is prepared to suffer the evil consequence from the supposed wrong doer out of good will and enters into a dialogue to change his heart.

> "Any reform" says Aldous Huxley, "which requires violence for its imposition will fail to produce good results. Violence can produce only the effects of violence - counter violence, suspicion, resentment, more violence. The effects of violence can be undone only by acts, of non-violence."[14]

Gandhi objects to violence because it appears to do good but the good it does to us is temporary and the evil it does is permanent.[15] Gandhi holds that man can go out of violence only through non-violence. Love alone can overcome hatred for hatred results in more hatred. Similar view is held by Lord Buddha:

> Never does hatred cease by hating but hatred ceases by love. This is the ancient law.[16]

The law established by Buddha is stated to be unalterable. For Gandhi, the atom bomb and all that it stands for are negation of non-violence. His firm conviction is that the peace established with the aid of the military or the police is not peace. True peace emanates from non-violence.[17] Gandhi claims that a state which relies on non-violence is capable of offering non-violent resistance against a world, combination based on armed-force. He conceives the non-violent resistance as the most powerful and effective than the military defense. Non-violence is rational and a mightier force than the armed force.

Gandhi holds that non-violence is:

> "a force mightier than the force of arms however powerful... The power that armaments give to defend right is nothing compared to the power that non-violence gives to do the same thing and that too with better show of reason."[18]

We cannot experience the real love in the absence of non-violence. Love is another name or the positive aspect of non-violence as it is the love of being.

> "If Peace" says Gandhi "is to be brought about by both parties being equally matched in the use of violence both offensive and defensive . . . It will be an armed peace to be broken at any moment."[19]

From the standpoint of Gandhi, states which use nuclear weapons can never be just and no value results from an atomic war.[20]

Human development is crippled because of the militarization of the scientific endeavour. Non-violent world order is realizable provided the immoral use of science that leads to destruction of the human race is eschewed. There is need for the observation of the ethic of science for creativity, cooperation and human progress.

Although there have been cataclysmic changes in the world. Gandhi adheres to his faith in truth and non-violence. They constitute the mightiest force at the disposal of mankind in the world. Atom bomb is of no effect before it. He emphasizes the need for the humanity to recognize this truth to escape from self-destruction.

> "The moral to be legitimately" says Gandhi, "drawn from the supreme tragedy of the bombs that it will not be destroyed by counter bombs even as violence cannot be overcome by counter-violence. Mankind has to get out of violence only through non-violence. Hatred can be over come only by love. Counter-hatred only increases the surface as well as the depth of hatred."[21]

There is need to shed the desire of exploitation and the spirit of violence for the peace to be established on this earth. Even after the World War II he continues to hold the same opinion:

> "I have no doubt", says Gandhi, "that unless big nations shed their desire of exploitation and the spirit of violence of which war is the natural expression and atom bomb, the inevitable. Consequence, there is no hope for peace in the world."[22]

Unless non-violence is made as the governing principle of the individual and social conduct in all the nations, world peace cannot be established.[23]

The Idea of World Government

There is need for the humanity to be built on the basis of internationalism transcending nationalism. This togetherness helps the mankind to evolve a moral and spiritual outlook for one world culture. Racialism and regionalism must be fought. Love for humanity should transcend, narrow attachment of geographical and political limits. Nations, races, tribes and states have to dissolve themselves to give vent to the formation of a wider humanity without the application of violent force which results in fear, bitterness and hatred defeating the very purpose of integration. The world has to be united and sustained only on a firm and unfaltering non-violent foundation.[24]

> "The world order" says Dr. Radhakrishnan, "we seek is not either national or continental. It is neither Eastern nor Western. It is universal."[25]

Realizing the importance of one world, Jawaharlal Nehru has pointed out that earnest efforts are being made to realize this ideal of human race as it has become so imperative today. If there is no world order then there might be no order at all left in the world.[26]

Bertrand Russell also realizes the need for the world government to have order and peace. He holds that a scientific society can be stable under certain conditions. The first condition is formation of a single government of the whole world with the monopoly of armed force which would be able to enforce peace. The second condition is the general diffusion of prosperity to avoid the possible jealousy and envy of one part of the world by the other. The third condition is the control over birth rate to have low birth rate everywhere. The fourth condition is the creation of conditions conducive to the individual to take initiative both at work and in play and the greatest diffusion of power compatible with maintaining the necessary political and economic framework. Until these conditions are fulfilled, a scientifically organized world will continue to reel uner certain grave risks.[27]

> "It is impossible" says Gandhi, "for one to be internationalist without being a nationalist. Internationalism is possible only when nationalism becomes a fact, i.e., when people belonging to different countries have organized themselves and are able to act as one man. It is not nationalism that is evil. It is the narrowness, selfish exclusiveness which is the bane of modern nations which is evil. Each wants to profit at the expense of the other and rise to ruin the other. India's nationalism, I hope struck a different path. It wants to organize itself or to find full self-expression for the benefit and service of humanity at large."[28]

The opinion of Gandhi that one cannot be on internationalist without being a nationalist is held by Immanuel Kant. He could see no prospect of one world-state or republic without establishing the local personal relationships among men in their nation states. He is very practical and realistic in hooking this opinion.

Gandhi holds that isolated independence is not the goal of the world states but a voluntary interdependence.[29] A federation of friendly interdependent states is desired by the better mind of today but not absolutely independent states warring against one another.[30] Interdependence ought to be the ideal of man in the absence of which man cannot realize his oneness with the universe.[31]

The union of ail hearts plays a pivotal role in establishing peace. Gandhi holds that even if the communal pacts are good, they are useless unless they are backed by the union of hearts and in its obscene there is no possibility to have peace on earth. This union can be brought about by mutual service and cooperative work.[32]

The piling up of mishear armaments creates new fears. Had Gandhi been alive, as Dr. Radhakrishnan pointed out, he would have liked to work out for general and complete disarmament and world peace.[33] The alternative to violent war is total disarmament and non-violent rearmament as there is no failure in a non-violent war.[34]

Some nations might embark on nuclear programmes to achieve military superiority while other nations think that peace can be established by relying on the doctrine of deterrence but there is no credible assurance to ensure lasting peace by relying on them.

War results when peace fails and the human effort should be directed towards peace.[35] The governing force that binds all humanity is love. This helps all to live together in peace. Gandhi holds that it is not force of arms that helps one another to be at peace but that of love and there is no better cement than that of love to be found in the world.[36]

Some might think that peace may be secured by diplomatic relations, negotiations, violence or armaments but the peace secured by the free advocacy of truth and non-violence is enduring and lasting.[37] Gandhi has realized that the nuclear proliferation and achieving military technology stand contrary to the vision of the non-violent world. Humanity has to invariably take the path that Gandhi has wanted us as there is no other alternative.

The practice of non-violence is life affirming which contributes to the human unity, progress and peace.

> "Through the universal practice of love" says Sorokin, "hatred, antagonism and injustice would be eliminated, and abiding harmony would prevail throughout the entire human universe."[38]

REFERENCES

1. V.K. Subrahmanyan, *Tr. Maxims of Chanakya*, p. 176.
2. *Ibid.*, p. 180.
3. *Harijan*, 16.5.1936. p. 109.
4. *Ibid.*, 17.11.1946. p. 404.
5. *Ibid.*, 24.12.1936. p. 345.
6. Niharranjan Roy (Ed), *Gandhi Theory and Practice: Social Impact and Contemporary Relevance*, p. 506.
7. Inozemtseve (Ed), *Global Problems of our Age*. p. 66,
8. *Ibid.*. p. 9.
9. K. Subrahmanyam (Ed), *Nuclear Myths and Realities*, pp. 52-53.
10. Dr. Vivek Ranjan Bhattacharya, *Indira Gandhi - Her Role in World Peace*, p. 88.
11. Text of the late Prime Minister Shri Rajiv Gandhi's address to the Third Special Session on Discernament of the United Nations General Assembly. p. 2.
12. Albert Schweitzer, *Peace or Atomic War*, p. 12-13
13. *Ibid.*, p. 24.
14. Aldous Huxley, *Ends and Means*. p. 9.
15. *Young India*, 26.2.1931., p. 1.
16. Dr. P.L. Vaidya (Tr.) *Buddha Dhammapada*, p. 53.
17. *Harijan*. 6.4.1947, p. 99.
18. *Ibid.*, 14.10.1939, p. 234.
19. *Ibid.*, 7.10.1939, p. 296
20. Paul F. Fower, *Gandhi on World Affairs*, p. 64.

21. *Harijan*, 7.7.1946, p. 212.
22. *Ibid.*, 10.11.1946, pp. 163-64.
23. *Gandhi Marg*, Vol. April 1982, p. 22.
24. George Kotturan, *Ahimsa – Gautama to Gandhi*, pp. 214-15.
25. S. Radhakrishnan, *Religion in a Chancing World*, p.23.
26. Jawaharlal Nehru, *India's Foreign Policy*, p. 182.
27. Bertrand Russell, *Impact of Science and Society*, pp. 1-30.
28. *Young India*, 18.6.1926, p. 211.
29. *Ibid.*,17.7.1924, p. 236.
30. *Ibid.*, 26.12.1924, p. 425.
31. *Ibid.*, 21.3.1929, p. 93.
32. *Harijan*, 25.1.1942, p. 13.
33. Pyarelal, *Mahatma Gandhi*, Vol. 1, p. X.
34. Jayaprakash Narayan's Speech of Tirupathi, *Peace News*, 12th July 1963.
35. *Harijan*, 12.1.1947, p. 248.
36. *Ibid.*, 25.1.1948, p. 535-36
37. Leo Tolstoy, *Christianity and Patriotism*, pp.533-39,
38. Petrim A. Sorokin, *Reconstruction of Humanity*, p.46.

13

Gandhian Philosophy and Its Relevance to the Modern Times

The lives of great men have shaped the destiny of the people through their enlightening teachings. They aroused moral consciousness among the people and contributed much to the progress of the nation.

When the country was ablaze with the conflagration of the foreign domination, Mahatma Gandhi through his weapon of Non-violence and *Satyagraha* set the nation free by arousing national consciousness.

Gandhi is held in high esteem being venerated as the Mahatma which implies the Great Soul, the father of the nation, and maker of modern India. The contribution he made to the national development and progress is outstanding and noteworthy.

Gandhi's sayings, 'My life is my message', and 'My life is a series of experiments with Truth'[1] are literally true. The words he uttered and spoke stand as the testament of his life. Poet Rabindranath Tagore eulogizing Mahatma Gandhi once said that the man was much more greater than all his writings and speeches. In the words of Jawaharlal Nehru, Gandhi lived the life of a supreme artist integrating in him the highest values of life-Truth, Beauty and Goodness and the values for which he stood are more relevant today than even before.

Looking at the traditional Indian society facing the challenges of his times generated by the confrontation of the foreign domination and colonialism on the one hand and weak, poor, disputed stratified social order on the other, involving himself in the tensions and turmoil's of our society had experienced, Gandhi felt the absolute need to ponder over the total situation by going to their very roots and ramifications through time. In the process he developed a world view for the well, being and welfare of humanity.

Mahatma Gandhi was essentially a man of action and he committed himself to the great task of the transformation of the Indian society in accordance with the social vision he had. The ideas he developed were conditioned by his experience, his insight, education and the teachings of the great masters like Tolstoy and John Ruskin had a profound influence on him. As an important aspect of his programme for the social reconstruction of the Indian society, he wanted to bring about a reform in the status and general living and social conditions of women in society. Although Gandhi was not opposed to the good things in the western way of life, or to the status of women in the western society, he opposed the irrational craze that had seized a section of Indian society form imitating the west when it did not suit the Indian society. He advised women to refuse to decorate themselves and not to go in for scents and lavender waters. If women want to give out fragrance, it must come of their heart. Thereby they can captivate not men but the humanity.[1]

For Gandhi the liberation of India was as necessary as the liberation of women. In his speeches and writings, he dealt at length with the problem of the regeneration of women.

> "Women" says Gandhi "is the companion of man, gifted with equal mental capacities. She has the right to participate in the minutest detail of the activities of man and she has the same right of freedom and liberty as he. She is entitled to a supreme place in her own sphere of activity as man is in his".[2]

Man and women are equal in status but they are not identical. Gandhi said that both should enjoy absolute equality in public life and women should suffer no legal disability and they are entitled to have from chase and equal legal status.

In a non-violent war against injustice, women could be co-shares. In a way women could make even greater contribution than men to a non-violent war if she could realize their strength.[3] Gandhi declared:

> To call woman the weaker sex is a libel; it is man's injustice to women If by strength is meant moral powers then woman is immeasurable man's superior.[4]

He pointed out that man should learn to give a proper place to women. A community or country in which women are not honored cannot be considered civilized.[5]

Gandhi was wedded to the work for the eradication of untouchability. He wished to be reborn an untouchable so that he may share their sorrows, sufferings and he may Endeavour to free them from that miserable condition.

> "I do not want to be reborn" says Gandhi, "But if I have to be reborn, I should be born an untouchable, so that may share their sorrows, sufferings and the affronts leveled against them in order that I may Endeavour to free myself and them from that miserable condition. I therefore prayed that I should be reborn again, I should do so not as a Brahmin, Kshatriya Vaishya or Shudra, but as a Atishudra".[6]

Gandhi upheld the inter-caste marriages and inter-dining. He stood against the dowry system. He said that the evil system of dowry must go. He stated that the system is intimately connected with taste. So long as the choice is restricted to a few hundred young men or women of a particular caste, the system will persist. The girls or boys or their parents have to break the bonds of caste to eradicate the evil. This is only education which builds character that will revolutionize the mentality of the youth of the nation.[7] Gandhi pointed out:

> Any young man who makes dowry a condition of marriage discredits his education, his country and dishonors womanhood... A strong public opinion should be created in condemnation of the degrading practice of dowry and young men who soil their frigers with such ill-gotten gold should be excommunicated from society.[8]

In our country not even a single day passes without the news in the papers mentioning about the brides who are set ablaze in some state or the other. These deaths reveal that behind these ghastly incidents, the prime cause is dowry.

Gandhi aimed at a total prohibition to. save the people from the evil. He held that the drink and drugs undermine the moral well-being. The lives is of those who drink are insecure. The evil caused by the drinks is infinitely worse than the evil caused by malaria and the like.

The alcoholic could be seen in a most pathetic condition. They waste all their earnings in drink and their lives become devoid of any grace. The lives of several princes were ruined because of liquor and the condition of labour who indulges in drink is pitiable. Gandhi pointed out:

> In a nutshell, alcohol are physically, socially, morally, intellectually and economically.[9]

Gandhi held that prohibition implies giving a new life for many millions. It is a new and substantial accession of moral and material strength. He felt that the voluntary organizations especially manned by women would work in the labour areas who could visit these who are addicted to drink and try to wean them from the habit.

The recent anti-arrack movement started by women has gained moral support from all corners. This movement is consonant with the aim and aspiration of Mahatma Gandhi.

Gandhi brought down religion from the cloistered seclusion of yogic contemplation to man's socio-political plane. For him there is no religion higher than Truth and righteousness. He said that 'as soon as we lose moral basis we cease to be religious'. His idea was to equate religion with morality and make religion dynamically operative in human life. He did not subscribe to the fanatic vie. That there one religion. For him the essence of all religions is one.

Everywhere in the world, individuals and groups are divided because of fear, suspicion, hatred and lack of mutual trust. The division may express itself on religious, economic, political or caste lines. Feeling of insecurity economic, political or caste perhaps is the major cause of these divisions. A person who is integrated fears none and consequently provokes no fear.

Gandhi teaches us to rise above fear, jealousy and hatred when individuals write, the problem of communal jealousy and discord would not arise.

Gandhi projected the universal human values preached by all major religions like Christianity, Hinduism, Islam, and hoped that in course of time the forces of unity would triumph over separatism for true religion could only unite but does no. Keep men separated because of their different faiths. If Hindus, Muslims and people ot other religions in India look upon themselves as essentially separate groups, the fault does not lie in the beliefs and practices enjoined by their scriptures but in a defective understanding of the real message.

While referring to the Hindu-Muslim unity, Gandhi said that it has been his passion since his childhood. The Hindu-Muslim unity consists in having a common purpose, a common goal and common sorrows. The unity is best promoted by sharing of one another's sorrows and by mutual toleration.[10] Gandhi pointed out:

> Hindu-Muslim unity means not unity only between Hindus and Musalmans, but between all those who believe India to be their home, no matter to what faith they belong.[11]

Gandhi measured development in terms of human progress and values. He did not stand against the entire spectrum of technology that is relevant to the human needs provided it does not erode the moral fibre of the society. Technology should be developed in order to sustain mankind without eroding human values.

The modern man is confronted with problems like environmental pollution, dehumanization and alienation. Technology should give scope for full employment without alienation and exploitation. Ecological balance should be maintained and rural urban disparities are to be reduced what is needed is appropriate technology and a technology with a human free.

Gandhi argued that we cannot build a non-violent society where economic production is concentrated in a few hands and where there is competition and greed.

Gandhi stood against the multiplication of wants. His wants could be reduced without loss. All wants are not indispensable. He is practical and right in saying that we have to subordinate our maternal life to higher ideals. In the Indian context, even from a realistic view point, Gandhian economic programme of village reconstruction and rejuvenation of village industries has gained importance and relevance.

There is no escape from hatred, violence and war if the nations do not practice non-violence. Non-violence aims at the human unity for it is the law of love and law of being which binds all people together.

The ancient Indian concept of non-violence is an expression of world and life negation without any aims set before it to be realized in this world. Gandhi places non-violence at the service of mankind in all the spheres of the human Endeavour.

Violence attacks not only the sin but also the sinner where as non-violence attacks only the sin. Non-violence is constructive in action and contributes to the real progress of the humanity but violence is destructive. Non-violence is followed by the acts of justice and good will but violence arouses emotions like hatred, fear and resentment. Violence cannot be quenched by superior violence but by non-violence. In this world, hatred is never ceased by hatred but by love. Violence indicates human in security.

Non-violence plays a dominant part in the world of nuclear proliferation and contributes the restoration of peace. Some nations embark or nuclear programmes to achieve military superiority while other nations think that peace can be established by relying on the doctrine of deterrence which responds in conditional basis and promotes mutual terror on the other hand. But there is no credible assurance to ensure lasting peace by relying on them. Had Gandhi been alive as Dr. S. Radhakrishnan pointed out, he would have liked to workout for general and complete disarmament. Even a few hours before death, Gandhi reaffirmed his faith, on non-violence and said that the weapon of non-violence alone could provide an answer to the challenge of nuclear weapons.

Human development is crippled because of the militarization of the scientific Endeavour. Peace promotes social justice. Some might think that peace may be secured by diplomatic relations, negotiations, violence are armaments but the peace secured by the free advocacy of truth and non-violence is enduring and lasting. Through the universal practice of love which is a positive aspect of non-violence hatred and injustice would be eliminated. Abiding harmony and peace would prevail. There by man could promote the supreme obligation of mutual concord and love.

REFERENCES

1. *Young India.* 8.12.1927. p.406.
2. *Speeches and Writings of Mahatma Gandhi,* p.4 25.
3. *Young India,* 14.1.1932, p. 19.
4. *Ibid.,* 10.4.1930, p.121
5. *Harijan,* 11.1.1948, p.508.
6. *Young India,* 4.5.19 21, p.144.
7. *Harijan,* 23.5.1936, p.117.
8. *Young India,* 21.6.19 29, p.207.
9. M.K. Gandhi, *Key to Health,* p.36.
10. *Young India,* 25.2.19 20, p.3.
11. *Ibid.,* 11.5.1921, p.148.

Bibliography

Adi, *Sarvodaya – A Political and Economic Study*. Asia Publishing House, Bombay, 1967.

Albert J. Peter, *We shall Overcome*. Pantheon Books, New York, 1990.

Bhattacharya, Vivek Ranjan, *Indira Gandhi - Her Role i World Peace*. New Delhi, Metropolitan Book Co.,1984.

Bose, N.K, *Selections from Gandhi*. Navajivan Publishir House, Ahmedabad, 1972.

Colaiaco A. James, *Martin Luther King Jr.: An Apostle Militant Non-violence*. Macmillan Academic a Professional Ltd., Hong Kong, 1990.

Chaiuhan, C.P.S., *Modern Indian Education Polic Progress and Problems*.

Carter V. Good, *Dictionary of Education*, McGraw-Hill Bk Company, New York, 1979, p. 420.

Dhavan, Gopinath, *The Political Philosophyof Mahat Gandhi*. Navaj ivan Publishing House, Ahmedabad,16

Datta, D.M., *The Philosophy of Mahatma Gandhi*. Univty of Wisconsin Press, Madison, 1953.

Datta D.K., *Social, Moral and Religious Philosop of Mahatna Gandhi. Intellectual Book Corner*, New hi, 1980.

Devaraja N.K., *Philosophy, Religion and Culture. Motilal Banarasidass*, Delhi, 1974.

Dewey, John, *Democracy and Education*, p. 324.

George, H. Sabine, *A Study of Political Theory*, p. 69.

Gisbert, Pascuel, *Fundamental of Sociology* (Orient Longmans, Bombay), p. 210.

Gandhi, M.K., *The Story of My Experiments with Truth*. Navajivan Publishing House, Ahmedabad, 1976.

Gandhi, M.K., *Ethical Religion* Tr. A. Ramiyers. Ganesan, Madras, 1922.

Gandhi, M.K., *Satyagraha*. Navajivan Publishing House, Ahmedabad, 1951.

Gandhi, M.K., *The Story of My Experiments with Truth*.

Gandhi, M.K., *Towards New Education*.

George, Kotturan, *Ahiṁsa - Gautama to Gandhi*. Sterling Publishers Pvt. Ltd., New Delhi, 1973.

Ghosh, Suresh Chandra. *The History of Education in Modern India*, 1757-1998, PP. 166-167.

Gopala Krishna, V., *New Facets of Eastern and Western Philosophy of Education*, pp. 1-2.

Hind Swaraj, Navajivan Publishing House, Ahmedabad, 1958.

Huxley Aldous, *Ends and Means*. Chatto and Windus, London, 1957.

Immanuel Kant, *Perpetual Peace – A Philosophical Essay*. The Liberal Arts Press, New York, 1948.

Inozentsev (Ed)., *Global Problems of Our Age*. Progress Publishers, Moscow, 1981.

John, J. Ausbro., Martin Luther King-J.R. The Making of a –Mind. Orbs Books, Mary Knoll, New York, 1982.

Joshi, S.C., *Gandhian Social Work,* Akansha, New Delhi, 2009

Lee C. Deighgton (ed), *Encyclopedia of Philosophy of Education*, p. 101, The Macmillan Company, USA., 1971.

Mahatma Gandhi, Government of India, New Delhi Publication Division, 1969.

Mathur, J. S. (ed), *Facets of Gandhian Thought*, p. 94.

Mandela Nelson, *Struggle is My Life.* Popular Prakashan Pvt. Ltd., Bombay, 1990.

Mathur, JS, *Facets of Gandhian Thought*, p. 95.

Narayan Jayaprakash, *Socialism – Sarvodaya and Democracy*. Asia Publishing House, Bombay, 1964.

Nehru, Jawaharlal, *India's Foreign Policy*. Government of India, New Delhi, 1981.

Pani, S. and Pani, Niranjan, *Reflections on Gandhi: The Forgotten Mahatma,* Zenith, Delhi, 2008.

Park, Joe (ed), *Selected Readings in the Philosophy of Education*, pp. 3-4.

Park, Joe (ed), *Selected Readings in the Philosophy of Education*, p. 5.

Pyarelal, *Mahatma Gandhi – Thus Last Phase* 2nd Vol. Navajivan Publishing House, Ahmedabad, 1956.

Pyarelal, *Mahatma Gandhi – The Early Phase* Vol. I Navajivan Press, Ahmedabad, 1963.

Radhakrishnan, S., *Religion in a Changing World*. George Allen & Unwin Ltd., London, 1977.

Ramachandran, (ed), *Quest for Gandhi*, pp. 332-334.

Russell, Bertrand, *Impact of Science and Society*. George Allen & Unwin Ltd., London, 1959.

Ruskin, John, *Unto This Last*. Oxford University Press, London 1923.

Singh, Ramjee, *Gandhi and the Modern World*, p. 224.

Sethe, J.D., *Gandhi Today*. Vikas Publishing House, New Delhi, 1973.

Singh, Ranjee, *Relevance of Gandhian Thought*. Classical Publishing Company, New Delhi, 1983.

Tolstoy, Leo, *Christianity and Patriotism*. Oxford University Press, London, -1960.

Vaidya, P.L., *Buddha Dhammapada* Tr. The Oriental Book Agency, Poona, 1934

Varma, K.H.P. (Ed), *Philosophy of Religion*. Classical Publishing Company, New Delhi, 1982.

Varna, V.P., *The Political Philosophy of Mahatna Gandhi, and Sarvodaya*. Lakshni Narain Agarwal, Agra,1972.

Journals

Gandhi Marg, Gandhi Smarak Nidhi, New Delhi.

Harijan, Harijan Sevak Sangh, Poona, Navajivan Trust, Ahmedabad.

Harijan (various issues).

Selections from Bose. pp. 251-256, 263-66

Mudaliar Commission, Secondary Education Commission Report, (1952-53), p. 24.

Young India, (various issues)

Encyclopedia

The Encyclopedia of Education. Preface, p. VIII.

Report of the Education Commission, p. 358

Index

■■■